## Instant & Interactive

# Math Picture Pages With Activities

### by Jacquelyn Johnson Howes

SCHOLASTIC
PROFESSIONAL BOOKS

**New York • Toronto • London • Auckland • Sydney
Mexico City • New Delhi • Hong Kong**

## Dedication

To my children, Rick, Tommy, Steve, and Betsy, for always encouraging me; to my friend and colleague, Jean Evans, for always supporting my creative efforts; and to Liza, Linda, Danielle, and Rebecca at Scholastic for their friendship and support. But most of all this book is dedicated to all children, who will understand math better by using this visual method.

Cover design by Jaime Lucero
Cover and interior artwork by Dana Regan,
except pages 42, 43, 56, 57, 62, and 98 by Rusty Fletcher
Interior design by Grafica, Inc.
Edited by Linda Ward Beech

ISBN: 0-439-07748-6
Copyright © 2000 by Jacquelyn Johnson Howes
All rights reserved.
Printed in the U.S.A.

# Contents

## Themes and Skills

# Contents

## Additional Materials

# Introduction

## What Is a Math Picture?

A math picture is a theme-based arrangement of specific numbers of characters or objects on a page. The purpose of a math picture is to provide children with a visual, concrete experience in exploring basic math concepts. In this book you'll find twelve thematic math pictures, each with accompanying math skill sheets. Six of the themes are curriculum-based, and six are seasonal themes. On each math picture, there are characters representing the amounts one through ten. For example, on the School Store math picture, there is one paint set, two notebook binders, three pads, and so on.

## Why Use Math Pictures?

Math pictures are fun, useful, visual, and effective. They provide a real and meaningful focus for your math lessons. Math pictures are great for visual learners and motivate all children to practice computation. Not only can you use math pictures to help children develop skills to meet the NCTM standards, but you can weave these lessons into theme units involving other curriculum areas as well. Because a math picture is interactive, children can see and do math using items in the arrangement. You can use the picture again and again, adapting it to the skill needs of your students or to explore new math concepts.

## What Math Concepts Can You Teach With Math Pictures?

With a math picture, you can have children work on addition, subtraction, graphing, multiplication, division, counting, measuring, applying money concepts, symmetry, and word problems. Use the skills matrix on page 6 as you develop your lesson plans. To make planning easier, each thematic chapter is listed on the left side of the matrix. The skills targeted within each chapter are represented in each column with stars.

| | Addition | Subtraction | Graphing | Counting | Multiplication | Division | Symmetry | Measuring | Word Problems | Money |
|---|---|---|---|---|---|---|---|---|---|---|
| School Store | ☆ | ☆ | ☆ | ☆ | | | | | | |
| Ocean Life | ☆ | ☆ | ☆ | | | | | | ☆ | |
| Halloween Party | ☆ | ☆ | ☆ | | | | | | ☆ | |
| Rain Forest | ☆ | ☆ | ☆ | ☆ | | | | | | |
| Autumn Harvest | ☆ | ☆ | | ☆ | | | | | | ☆ |
| Transportation | ☆ | ☆ | | ☆ | | | | | ☆ | |
| Holiday Toy Shop | ☆ | ☆ | ☆ | | | | | | | ☆ |
| Food Pyramid | ☆ | ☆ | | | ☆ | | | | ☆ | ☆ |
| Snow Sports | ☆ | ☆ | | | ☆ | | | | ☆ | |
| Dinomathic Park | ☆ | | | | ☆ | ☆ | | ☆ | ☆ | |
| Insects | ☆ | | | | | | ☆ | ☆ | ☆ | |
| Pleasant Pond Park | ☆ | ☆ | | | | | | ☆ | ☆ | |

## What Else Can You Teach With Math Pictures?

The math pictures in this book are based on high-interest curriculum and seasonal themes. By using these themes for math, you are also broadening children's knowledge of subjects important in science, social studies, and literature.

## Enlarging the Math Picture

You can reproduce the math picture on standard size (8 1/2" X 11") copy paper, or set your copy machine to enlarge 130% and use 12" X 18" paper.

## How Can You Adapt Math Pictures to Meet Children's Needs?

You can use the mini-characters on pages 93-94 and the blank concept sheets to create math sheets that meet the needs of your class.

## Teaching Addition With Math Pictures

Children can easily count on the picture how many of one character plus how many of another, because it is right in front of them.

Instant & Interactive Math Picture Pages With Activities
Scholastic Professional Books

## Teaching Subtraction With Math Pictures and Plastic Counters

Children who have difficulty with subtraction can easily place the amount of counters for the lower number on the characters representing the higher number. For example, if the problem is "eight manatees minus three sea lions," the child writes the numbers on the worksheet, then takes three plastic counters and places them on three of the eight manatees. The child then counts the remaining five manatees to obtain the answer.

## Creating Your Own Math Word Problems

Both you and your students will enjoy creating your own math word problems. When teaching children to create word problems, be sure to discuss key phrases in math problems:

How many____ are there all together?

How many ____ are there in all?

How many more _____ are there than _____?

How many fewer_____ are there than _____?

If (number) of ____ went away, how many would be left?

Be sure that children write the word that describes the two items that they are adding. For example, if they are adding seven scissors and eight erasers: How many supplies are there all together? If children are adding totally unlike things such as skis and penguins: How many winter items are there all together?

## Teaching Money Skills

Put price tags on characters in any of the math pictures to teach money skills.

## Making the Math Picture Into a Math Bulletin Board Mural

To make the characters larger, simply enlarge them to the desired size. Reproduce the same number of each character that appears on the math picture. You can use any size bulletin board, chalkboard, or white board for a math mural. If you have a magnetic chalkboard or white board, glue a small magnet to the back of each character. This enables you to reposition each character to set up different problems.

**Tip**

On page 101 are lists of the items (and how many there are) for each theme picture. You'll find these lists handy when working with the pictures.

# School Store

## Thoughts on the Theme

The School Store math picture and theme is a perfect way to launch the school year and show your students that math is fun. The math picture also provides an opportunity to talk about the use and care of the various materials and tools children will work with during the year.

Make a copy of the School Store theme picture for each child. Have children identify the items that are for sale.

## Using the Worksheets

Make copies of the worksheets that you want children to complete. Read the directions to the class and model how to do the first item.

@ **School Store Counting and Number Practice** is a good way to help reacquaint children with counting and writing numbers after the long summer vacation. Be sure children understand that they should count the number of the pictured item in the math picture and match that number to the numeral on the page. For extra practice, have children trace the other numbers in each row with a pencil.

@ **School Store Graphing** requires children to find and count each type of school supply and to match that number with the numeral on the page. Remind children to use a different color to make each bar of the graph.

@ **School Store Addition** requires children to count and then write the correct numbers to create the addition problems that they will solve. Point out that because children are adding unlike things, they should express their answers as "pads and markers" or "school supplies."

**School Store Subtraction** also requires children to count the items and write the correct numbers to create the problems that they will solve. Since children are subtracting unlike items, they should express their answers as "more crayons than markers" or "school supplies."

## More Math Ideas

**1.** Use the math picture to generate word problems. For example, you might ask:

- How many children can buy a box of crayons? How do you know?

- Eight children need scissors. Can they all buy a pair? How do you know?

- Five students need glue. Can they all buy a bottle? How do you know?

**2.** You might also have children add a price for each item in the picture and then solve problems using money.

**3.** Have children cut out ads for school supplies in local newspapers. Then teach a mini-lesson on comparative shopping.

## Math and Writing

Use the math picture to generate writing ideas. For example, have children:

- Write about a pencil that has trouble doing subtraction problems. What happens to the owner in math class?

- Write a set of directions on how to use one of the items in the school store. This may help children to develop respect for school supplies.

## Cross-Curriculum Bonus

*Social Studies:* Discuss what kinds of school supplies were used in Colonial times and one hundred years ago.

## Bookshelf Suggestions

- *Miss Nelson Is Missing!* by Harry Allard (Houghton Mifflin, 1985)

- *Franklin Goes to School* by Paulette Bourgeois and Brenda Clark (Kids Can Press, 1995)

- *A Little Shopping* by Cynthia Rylant (Aladdin, 2000)

- *Nobody's Mother Is in Second Grade* by Robin Pulver (Penguin Putnam, 1992)

- *My Teacher Sleeps in School* by Leatie Weiss (Penguin Putnam, 1985)

*Instant & Interactive Math Picture Pages With Activities*
Scholastic Professional Books

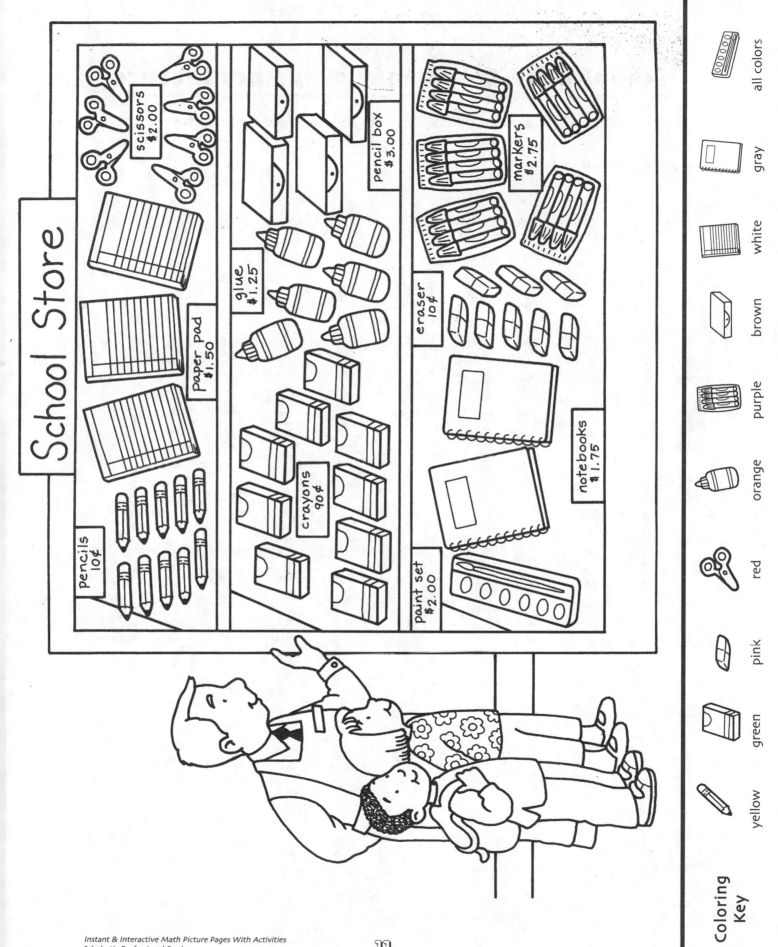

Instant & Interactive Math Picture Pages With Activities
Scholastic Professional Books

# School Store Counting and Number Practice

Use the math picture to count each thing you can buy. Trace that number with a crayon. Be sure to start at the top of the number. Then, take your pencil and trace the other numbers in the row.

1 2 3 4 5 6 7 8 9 10

1 2 3 4 5 6 7 8 9 10

1 2 3 4 5 6 7 8 9 10

1 2 3 4 5 6 7 8 9 10

1 2 3 4 5 6 7 8 9 10

1 2 3 4 5 6 7 8 9 10

1 2 3 4 5 6 7 8 9 10

1 2 3 4 5 6 7 8 9 10

1 2 3 4 5 6 7 8 9 10

1 2 3 4 5 6 7 8 9 10

*Instant & Interactive Math Picture Pages With Activities*
Scholastic Professional Books

# School Store Graphing

Use the math picture to count each thing you can buy at the school store. Color the graph to show that number. Use a different color for each bar.

**10**
**9**
**8**
**7**
**6**
**5**
**4**
**3**
**2**
**1**

# School Store Addition

Use the math picture to count and write the number in each box.  Add the numbers.

**1.**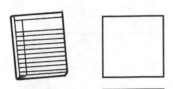

☐
☐
+

☐

**2.**

☐
☐
+

☐

**3.**

☐
☐
+

☐

**4.**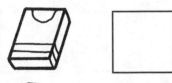

☐
☐
+

☐

**5.**

☐
☐
+

☐

**6.**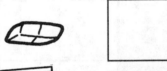

☐
☐
+

☐

**7.**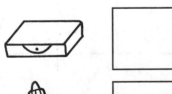

☐
☐
+

☐

**8.**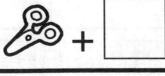

☐
☐
+

☐

**9.**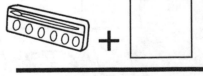

☐
☐
+

☐

*Instant & Interactive Math Picture Pages With Activities*
Scholastic Professional Books

# School Store Subtraction

Use the math picture to count and write the number in each box. Subtract the numbers.

**1.**

☐

☐ — ☐

_____

☐

**2.**
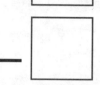
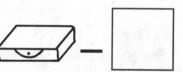

☐

☐ — ☐

_____

☐

**3.**

☐

☐ — ☐

_____

☐

**4.**

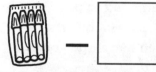

☐

☐ — ☐

_____

☐

**5.**

☐

☐ — ☐

_____

☐

**6.**

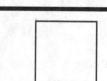

☐

☐ — ☐

_____

☐

**7.**

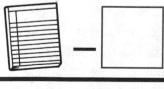

☐

☐ — ☐

_____

☐

**8.**

☐

☐ — ☐

_____

☐

**9.**

☐

☐ — ☐

_____

☐

# Ocean Life

## Thoughts on the Theme

Children are fascinated by ocean life, and this math picture is a perfect way for students to expand their knowledge of sea animals while they practice math skills.

Make a copy of the Ocean Life theme picture for each child. Review the names of each animal with the class: *lobster, octopus, manatee, dolphin, porpoise, walrus, shark, sea lion, seal,* and *killer whale.*

## Using the Worksheets

Make copies of the worksheets that you want students to complete. Read the directions to the class and model how to do the first item.

- ◉ **Ocean Life Graphing** requires finding and counting each type of sea creature, then matching the number with the correct numeral on the page. Remind children to use a different color to make each bar of the graph.

- ◉ **Ocean Life Addition** requires children to count and then write the correct numbers to create the addition problems that they will solve. Point out that because children are adding unlike sea animals, they should express their answers as "ocean animals."

- ◉ **Ocean Life Subtraction** also requires children to count the number of sea animals and write the correct numbers to create the problems that they will solve. Since children are subtracting unlike animals, they should express their answers as "more dolphins than seals" or "ocean animals."

*Instant & Interactive Math Picture Pages With Activities*
Scholastic Professional Books

@ For the **Ocean Life Questions** page, write the name of each animal on the chalkboard. Instruct children to write one name on each blank line. Then have children exchange papers with a partner and use the math picture to solve the problems. Remind children to add "s" if necessary for plural nouns.

## More Math Ideas

**1.** Use the Ocean Life picture for a measuring lesson. Using inches or centimeters, measure the distance between the animals, or measure the length of the ocean floor on the picture.

**2.** Present a lesson on the concepts of > greater than, and < less than. For example, the number of manatees is greater than the number of walruses, because 8>5.

## Math and Writing

Use the math picture to generate writing ideas. For example, have children:

@ Generate a list of questions involving number facts about the sea creatures such as: How many miles can a dolphin swim in a day? Encourage children to find and write the answers to one or more questions to share with the class.

@ Write word problems for each kind of animal. For example: We each have eight arms. There are nine of us in the picture. How many arms do we have in all?

## Cross-Curriculum Bonus

*Science:* Teach a lesson on the differences between mammals and fish. If possible, visit a local aquarium. Prepare questions to research beforehand.

## Bookshelf Suggestions

@ *The Magic School Bus on the Ocean Floor* by Joanna Cole (Scholastic, 1994)

@ *Nine True Dolphin Stories* by Margaret Davidson (Scholastic, 1990)

@ *The Desert Beneath the Sea* by Ann McGovern (Scholastic, 1991)

@ *The Ocean Alphabet Book* by Jerry Pallotta (Scholastic, 1990)

@ *The Sea* (The World Around Us series) by Brian Williams (Kingfisher Books, 1992)

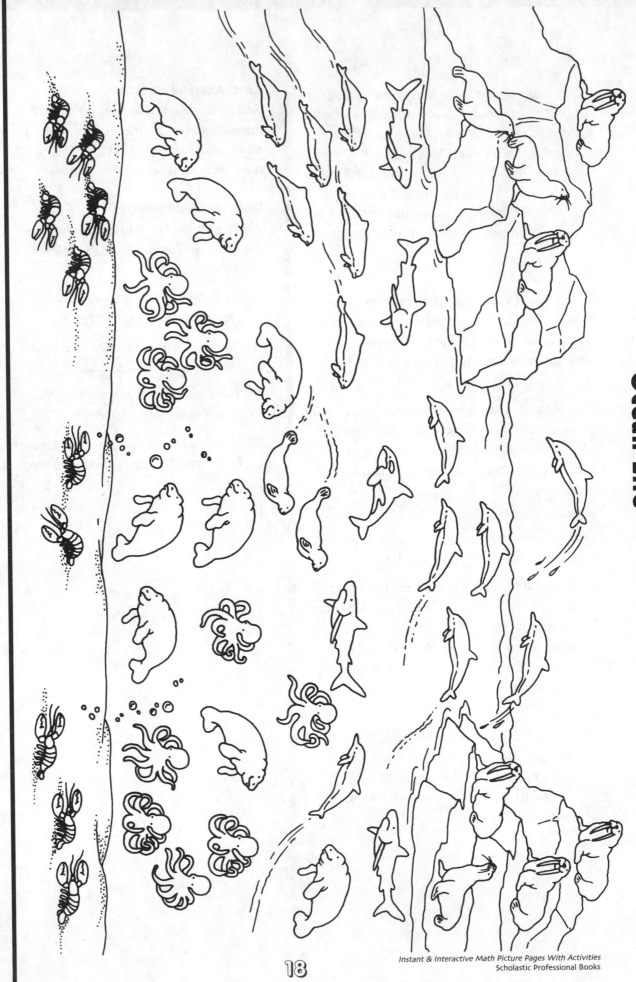

# Ocean Life

## Coloring Key

dark blue

pink

dark gray

light gray

light blue

dark brown

white

brown

peach

black

*Instant & Interactive Math Picture Pages With Activities*
Scholastic Professional Books

# Ocean Life Graphing

Use the math picture to count the number of each ocean animal. Color the graph to show how many of each animal you count. Use a different color for each bar.

| 10 | | | | | | | | | |
|---|---|---|---|---|---|---|---|---|---|
| 9 | | | | | | | | | |
| 8 | | | | | | | | | |
| 7 | | | | | | | | | |
| 6 | | | | | | | | | |
| 5 | | | | | | | | | |
| 4 | | | | | | | | | |
| 3 | | | | | | | | | |
| 2 | | | | | | | | | |
| 1 | | | | | | | | | |

# Ocean Life Addition

Use the math picture to count and write the number in each box. Add the numbers.

**1.**  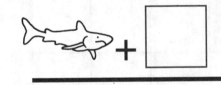 +

**2.**   +

**3.**  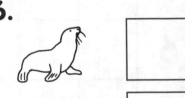 +

**4.**    +

**5.**  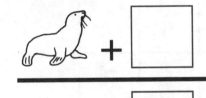 +

**6.**   +

**7.** 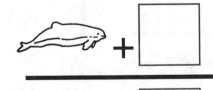 +

**8.** +

**9.**  +

*Instant & Interactive Math Picture Pages With Activities*
Scholastic Professional Books

# Ocean Life Subtraction

Use the math picture to count and write the number in each box.  Subtract the numbers.

**1.**

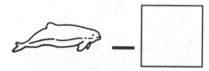 ▢ ▢ ▢

**2.**

 ▢ ▢ ▢

**3.**

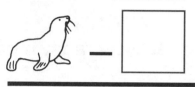 ▢ ▢ ▢

**4.**

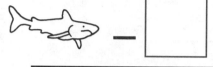

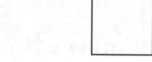 ▢ ▢ ▢

**5.**

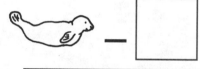

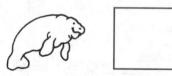 ▢ ▢ ▢

**6.**

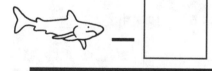 ▢ ▢ ▢

**7.**

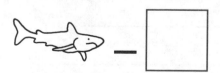 ▢ ▢ ▢

**8.**

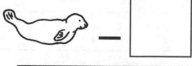 ▢ ▢ ▢

**9.**

 ▢ ▢ ▢

# Ocean Life Questions

Write the name of an ocean animal on each blank line. Change papers with a classmate to solve the problems.

**1.** How many _____ and _____ are there in all?

_____

**2.** How many more _____ are there than _____ ?

_____

**3.** Two of the _____ swim away. How many of them are left?

_____

**4.** How many _____ and _____ and _____ are there

in all? _____

**5.** How many sea animals are there in all? _____

**6.** Write a word problem of your own. _____

_____

_____

_____

_____

_____

Instant & Interactive Math Picture Pages With Activities
Scholastic Professional Books

# Halloween Party

## Thoughts on the Theme

Halloween is an exciting time for children, and they will look forward to doing math with the Halloween Party theme picture. If you have some children who do not celebrate Halloween, consider having them work on the Autumn Harvest math picture at this time.

Make a copy of the Halloween Party theme picture for each child. Have children identify the characters and talk about what they are doing at the Halloween Party.

## Using the Worksheets

Make copies of the worksheets that you want students to complete. Read the directions to the class and model how to do the first item.

**Halloween Party Graphing** requires children to find and count each type of character and to match that number to a numeral on the graph. Remind children to use a different color to make each bar of the graph.

**Halloween Party Addition** requires children to count and then write the correct numbers to create the addition problems that they will solve. Point out that because children are adding unlike characters, they should express their answers as "Halloween characters."

**Halloween Party Subtraction** also requires children to count the characters and write the correct numbers to create the problems that they will solve. Since children are subtracting unlike characters, they should express their answers as "more witches than pumpkins" or "Halloween characters."

@ For **Halloween Party Problems**, children should also refer to the math picture. Remind them to express their answers to reflect the characters that they are adding or subtracting.

## More Math Ideas

**1.** Use the math picture to generate word problems. For example, you might say:

@ Ten ghosts were invited to the party. How many ghosts did not come?

@ The skeletons danced with the witches. How many witches did not have a partner?

**2.** Use the Halloween Party house for a measuring lesson. Using inches or centimeters, have children measure the size of the rooms, the stairs, the characters, the entire height of the house.

**3.** Present a lesson on the concepts of > greater than, and < less than. For example, the number of witches is greater than the number of spiders, because 9>7.

## Math and Writing

Use the math picture to generate writing ideas. For example, have children:

@ Write clues to help a viewer find some of the Halloween guests in the house. For example: I wear no clothes, but I am in a closet. Who am I?

@ Make up poems based on the numbers of guests in the house. Example:

> Ten bats flew around
> While six ghosts ran up and down.

## Cross-Curriculum Bonus

*Science:* Have children choose one of these animals to learn about: bat, mouse, spider, owl.

## Bookshelf Suggestions

Here are some favorite Halloween books to use for reading and follow-up writing assignments:

@ *The Biggest Pumpkin Ever* by Jeni Bassett (Cartwheel Books, 1993)

@ *The Witch Goes To School* by Norman Bridwell (Scholastic, 1992)

@ *Stellaluna* by Janell Cannon (Harcourt Brace, 1993)

@ *Big Pumpkin* by Erica Silverman (Aladdin, 1995)

@ *Nate the Great and the Halloween Hunt* by Marjorie Weinman Sharmat (Young Yearling, 1990)

*Instant & Interactive Math Picture Pages With Activities*
Scholastic Professional Books

# Halloween Party

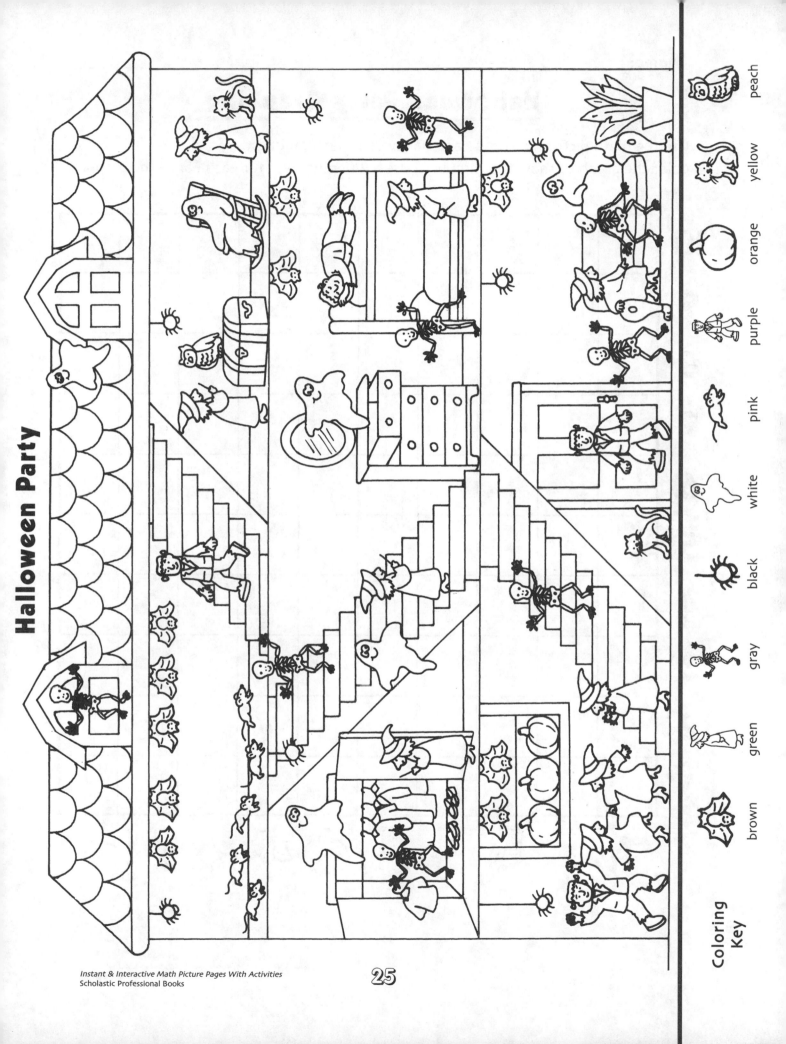

*Instant & Interactive Math Picture Pages With Activities*
Scholastic Professional Books

## Coloring Key

| | |
|---|---|
| peach | |
| yellow | |
| orange | |
| purple | |
| pink | |
| white | |
| black | |
| gray | |
| green | |
| brown | |

# Halloween Party Graphing

Use the math picture to count each Halloween character guest.
Color the graph to show that number.  Use a different color for each bar of the graph.

| **10** | | | | | | | | | | |
|---|---|---|---|---|---|---|---|---|---|---|
| **9** | | | | | | | | | | |
| **8** | | | | | | | | | | |
| **7** | | | | | | | | | | |
| **6** | | | | | | | | | | |
| **5** | | | | | | | | | | |
| **4** | | | | | | | | | | |
| **3** | | | | | | | | | | |
| **2** | | | | | | | | | | |
| **1** | | | | | | | | | | |

*Instant & Interactive Math Picture Pages With Activities*
Scholastic Professional Books

# Halloween Party Addition

Use the math picture to count and write the number in each box. Add the numbers.

**1.**

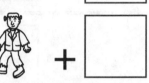

+

**2.**

+

**3.**

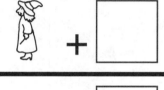

+

**4.**
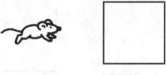
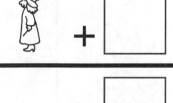

+

**5.**
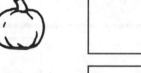

+

**6.**

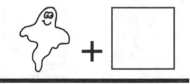
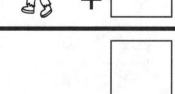

+

Name: _____

# Halloween Party Subtraction

Use the math picture to count and write the number in each box. Subtract the numbers.

1.
 — ☐
☐
_____
☐

2.
 — ☐
☐
_____
☐

3.
 — ☐
☐
_____
☐

4.
 — ☐
☐
_____
☐

5.
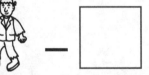 — ☐
☐
_____
☐

6.
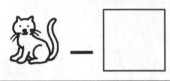 — ☐
☐
_____
☐

7.
 — ☐
☐
_____
☐

8.
 — ☐
☐
_____
☐

9.
 — ☐
☐
_____
☐

*Instant & Interactive Math Picture Pages With Activities*
Scholastic Professional Books

# Halloween Party Problems

Solve the problems. Use the math picture to help you.

1.  If the witches came on three brooms and the same number of witches rode on each broom, how many witches rode on each broom? _____ witches

2.  The ghosts were invited to ride along with the witches. If the same number of ghosts rode on each broom, how many ghosts would be on each broom? _____ ghosts  How many witches and ghosts rode together on each broom? _____ witches and _____ ghosts

3.  Count by twos to find out how many witch shoes there are in the picture. Don't forget each witch has two shoes, even though you can only see one shoe if she is standing sideways. Also include the shoes in the closet in your count. _____ shoes

4.  To play a Halloween game, the witches and Frankensteins made up one team. How many members were on their team? _____ The ghosts and skeletons made up the other team. How many were on their team? _____ Whose team will YOU have to join, so both teams have the same number of players? _____

5.  How many spiders are on each floor? First _____ Second _____ Third _____ How many spiders are there in all?

6.  How many more bats are there on the third floor than the first floor? _____

# Rain Forest

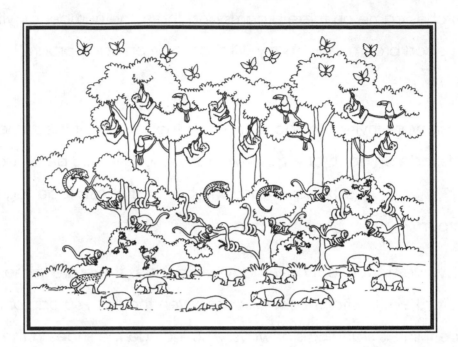

## Thoughts on the Theme

The numerous and exotic animals of the rain forest are an intriguing topic for children. With this math picture, they not only learn about the animal life, but the levels in the rain forest as well: the *emergent* level, the *canopy*, the *understory*, and the *floor*.

Make a copy of the Rain Forest theme picture for each child. Discuss each level of the rain forest and why it is a good place for each of the animals to live. Be sure that children know the names of each animal before they begin to do the math. The animals are: *jaguar, anteater, lizard, frog, toucan, snake, sloth, howler monkey, tapir,* and *butterfly*.

## Using the Worksheets

Make copies of the worksheets that you want students to complete. Read the directions to the class and model how to do the first item.

@ **Rain Forest Graphing** requires children to find and count each type of animal, then to match that number with the correct numeral on the graph. Remind children to use a different color to make each bar of the graph.

@ **Rain Forest Addition** requires children to count and then write the correct numbers to create the addition problems that they will solve. Point out that because children are adding unlike animals, they should express their answers as "rain forest animals."

*Instant & Interactive Math Picture Pages With Activities*
Scholastic Professional Books

Similarly, **Rain Forest Subtraction** calls for children to count the number of animals and write the correct numbers to create the problems that they will solve. Since children are subtracting unlike animals, they should express their answers as "more tapirs than toucans" or "rain forest animals."

**Counting by Twos & Fours** requires children to practice and review the skill of skip counting by twos in order to determine the number of legs on the animals pictured. This page provides a good visual multiplication lesson because each of these animals has four legs.

## More Math Ideas

**1.** Use the math picture to generate word problems. For example, you might say:

If four frogs and three lizards are eating in the understory, how many animals are eating there in all?

How many animals in all are in the canopy?

How many more tapirs than anteaters are on the forest floor?

**2.** Use the Rain Forest picture for a measuring lesson. Using inches or centimeters, have children measure the distance from one animal to another.

## Math and Writing

Use the math picture to generate writing ideas. For example, have children:

Explore large numbers by contributing to a class book of rain forest facts such as: Some rain forests get more than 400 inches of rain a year. We get _____ inches in our own region.

Write dialogue between two rain forest animals in the math picture.

## Cross-Curriculum Bonus

*Social Studies/Geography:* Where are the rain forests of the world? What countries have rain forests? What jobs are dependent upon the rain forest? Discuss how recycling ties in with studies about the rain forest and protecting the global environment.

## Bookshelf Suggestions

*The Great Kapok Tree* by Lynne Cherry (Voyager, 2000)

*Rain Forest* by Helen Cowcher (Sunburst, 1990)

*Here Is the Tropical Rain Forest* by Madeleine Dunphy (Hypherion, 1997)

*At Home in the Rain Forest* by Diane Willow (Charlesbridge, 1992)

*Welcome to the Green House* by Jane Yolan (Putnam, 1997)

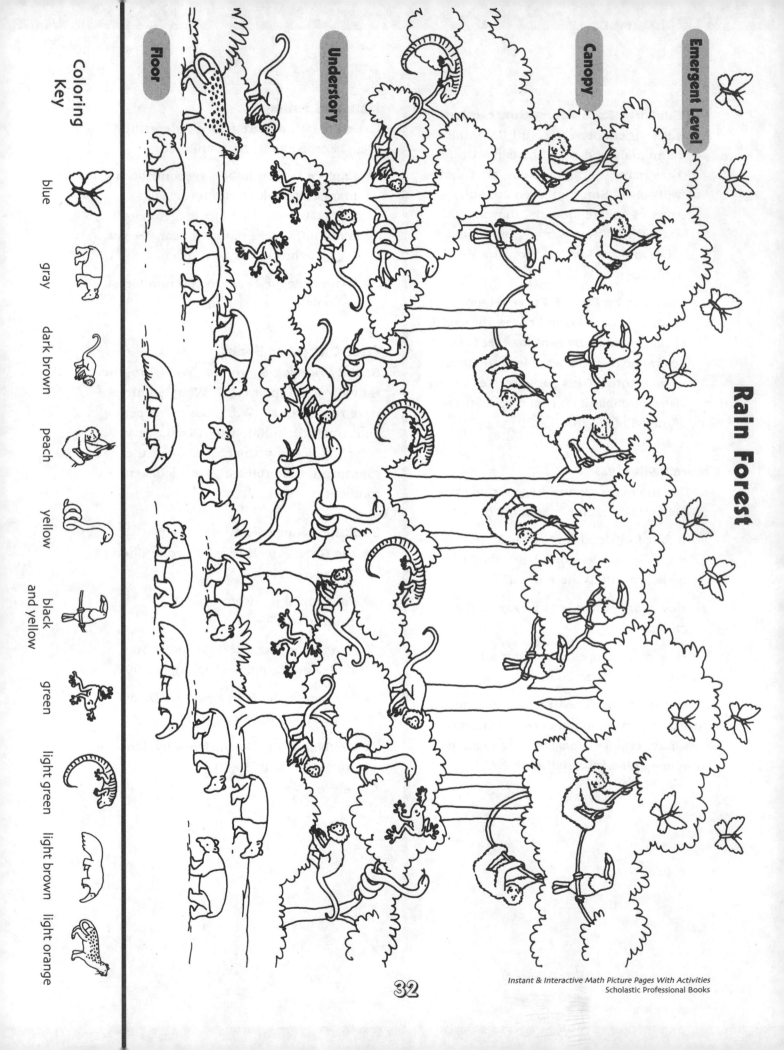

# Rain Forest

**Emergent Level**

**Canopy**

**Understory**

**Floor**

## Coloring Key

blue

gray

dark brown

peach

yellow

black and yellow

green

light green

light brown

light orange

*Instant & Interactive Math Picture Pages With Activities*
Scholastic Professional Books

# Rain Forest Graphing

Use the math picture to count each kind of animal.
Color the graph to show that number. Use a different color for each bar of the graph.

| 10 | | | | | | | | | | |
|----|---|---|---|---|---|---|---|---|---|---|
| 9  | | | | | | | | | | |
| 8  | | | | | | | | | | |
| 7  | | | | | | | | | | |
| 6  | | | | | | | | | | |
| 5  | | | | | | | | | | |
| 4  | | | | | | | | | | |
| 3  | | | | | | | | | | |
| 2  | | | | | | | | | | |
| 1  | | | | | | | | | | |

Name: _____

# Rain Forest Addition

Use the math picture to count and write the number in each box. Add the numbers.

**1.**
 +

☐
☐
────
☐

**2.**
 +

☐
☐
────
☐

**3.**
 +

☐
☐
────
☐

**4.**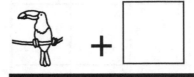
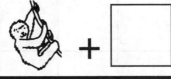 +

☐
☐
────
☐

**5.**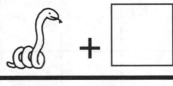
 +

☐
☐
────
☐

**6.**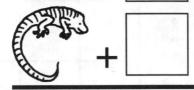
 +

☐
☐
────
☐

**7.**
 +

☐
☐
────
☐

**8.**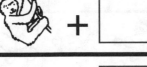
 +

☐
☐
────
☐

**9.**
 +

☐
☐
────
☐

Instant & Interactive Math Picture Pages With Activities
Scholastic Professional Books

Name: _____

# Rain Forest Subtraction

Use the math picture to count and write the number in each box. Subtract the numbers.

**1.**

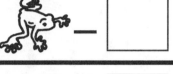

□

□ _ □

—

□

**2.**

□

□ _ □

—

□

**3.**

□

□ _ □

—

□

**4.**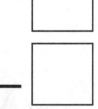

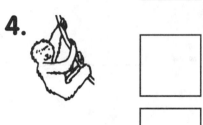

□

□ _ □

—

□

**5.**

□

□ _ □

—

□

**6.**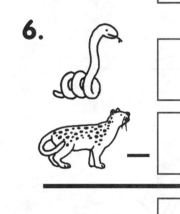

□

□ _ □

—

□

**7.**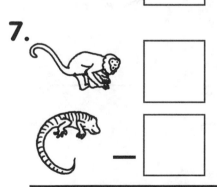

□

□ _ □

—

□

**8.**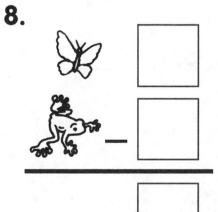

□

□ _ □

—

□

**9.**

□

□ _ □

—

□

*Instant & Interactive Math Picture Pages With Activities*
Scholastic Professional Books

# Rain Forest Counting by Twos & Fours

Practice counting by twos: 2  4  6  8  10  12
Practice counting by fours: 4  8  12  16  20  24

Using the math picture, count animal legs by twos or fours. Touch your fingertip to each set of legs as you count. How many (animal) legs are there all together? Write your answer on the line beneath the animals pictured below.

1. _____

2. _____

3. _____

4. _____

5. _____

6. _____

Instant & Interactive Math Picture Pages With Activities
Scholastic Professional Books

# Autumn Harvest

## Thoughts on the Theme

Celebrate the changes of fall with the Autumn Harvest math picture. This picture also provides an opportunity to talk about fall customs such as hayrides, state fairs, harvest festivals, and traditional autumn produce such as pumpkins and apples.

Make a copy of the Autumn Harvest theme picture for each child. Have children identify each item in the picture.

## Using the Worksheets

Make copies of the worksheets that you want students to complete. Read the directions to the class and model how to do the first item.

- For **Autumn Harvest Addition**, children count and then write the correct numbers to create the addition problems that they will solve. Point out that because children are adding unlike things, they should express their answers as "Autumn things" or "Autumn items."

- For **Autumn Harvest Subtraction**, children count the items and write the correct numbers to create the problems that they will solve. Again, children should express their answers as "more apples than cider" or "Autumn items."

- **Autumn Harvest Counting Money** requires children to identify coins and count the needed change to purchase items at the roadside stand. Review the cents and dollar signs if necessary.

- ☙ **Autumn Harvest Spending** allows children to "go shopping" and make their own choices of what to buy at the stand. Children will need red, blue and black crayons to complete this page.

## More Math Ideas

**1.** Use the math picture to generate word problems. For example, you might ask:

- ☙ How many people can buy a jug of cider? How do you know?

- ☙ Mrs. Woods bought all the apples and all the pies. How many things did she buy?

- ☙ Loretta has one dollar. How many hayrides can she have?

**2.** Bring in fall produce such as apples, pumpkins, and squash and conduct a lesson in comparing sizes and weights.

## Math and Writing

Use the math picture to generate writing ideas. For example, have children:

- ☙ Write about the biggest and smallest pumpkins in a farmer's field.

- ☙ Write about a hayride. Tell how many stops it makes, how many children are on it, and how long it takes.

- ☙ Write about designing a jack-o'-lantern face using only geometric shapes.

## Cross-Curriculum Bonus

*Art:* Make nature collages using autumn leaves, sponge painted leaves, or crayon rubbings of leaves.

## Bookshelf Suggestions

Here are some favorite fall books for reading and follow-up writing assignments:

- ☙ *How Do You Know It's Fall?* By Alan Fowler (Children's Press, 1994)

- ☙ *Ox Cart Man* by Donald Hall (Viking, 1983)

- ☙ *Picking Apples and Pumpkins* by Amy and Richard Hutchings (Cartwheel, 1994)

- ☙ *Why Do Leaves Change Color?* By Betsy Maestro (HarperTrophy, 1994)

- ☙ *I Am A Leaf* by Jean Marzollo (Cartwheel, 1999)

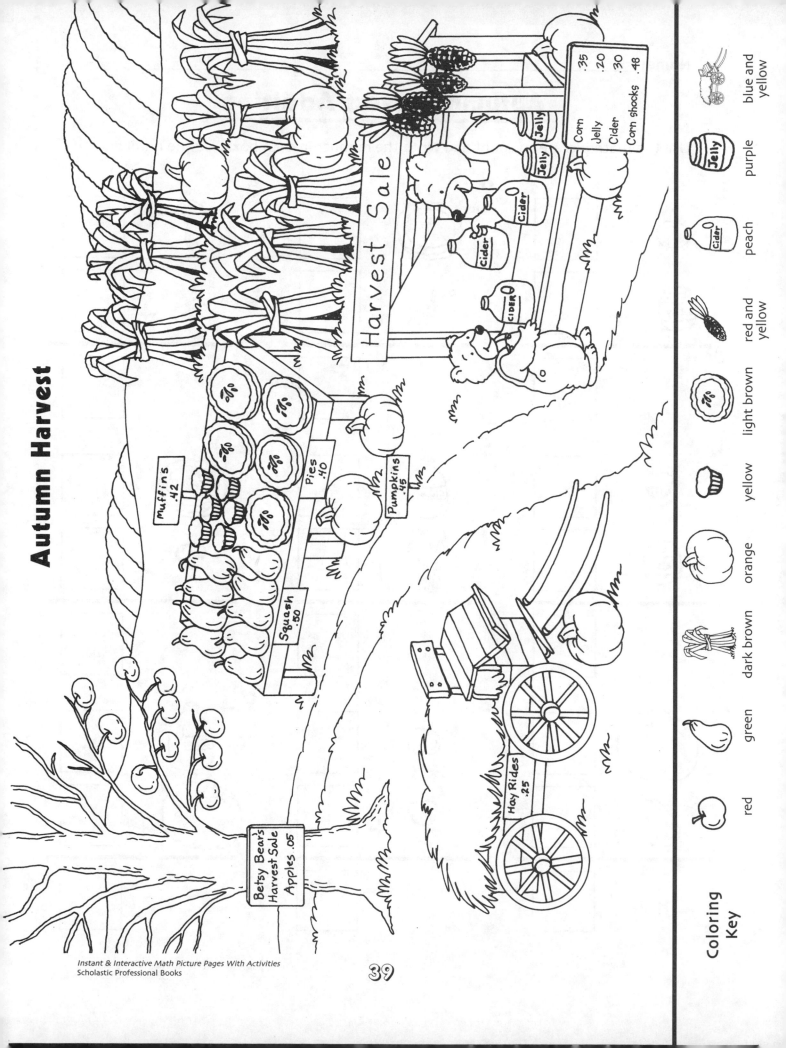

# Autumn Harvest

Harvest Sale

| Corn | .35 |
| Jelly | .20 |
| Cider | .30 |
| Corn shocks | .48 |

Jelly
Jelly
Jelly
Cider
Cider
Cider
CIDER

Muffins .42

Pies .40

Squash .50

Pumpkins .45

Betsy Bear's Harvest Sale Apples .05

Hay Rides .25

## Coloring Key

| | | |
|---|---|---|
| red | green | dark brown |
| orange | yellow | light brown |
| red and yellow | peach | purple |
| blue and yellow | | |

*Instant & Interactive Math Picture Pages With Activities*
Scholastic Professional Books

**Name:** _____

# Autumn Harvest Addition

Use the math picture to count and write the number in each box. Add the numbers.

**1.**   +

**2.**  +

**3.**  +

**4.** +

**5.** +

**6.**  +

**7.** 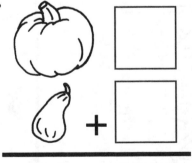 +

**8.**  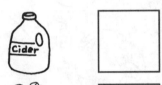 +

**9.**  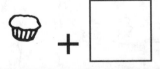 +

*Instant & Interactive Math Picture Pages With Activities*
Scholastic Professional Books

# Autumn Harvest Subtraction

Use the math picture to count and write the number in each box. Subtract the numbers.

**1.**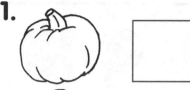

□

 − □

□

**2.**

□

 − □

□

**3.**

□

 − □

□

**4.**

□

 − □

□

**5.** 

□

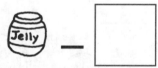 − □

□

**6.**

□

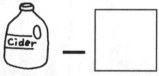 − □

□

**7.**

□

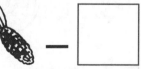 − □

□

**8.**

□

 − □

□

**9.**

□

 − □

□

# Autumn Harvest Counting Money

Circle the coins that you need to pay for each thing.

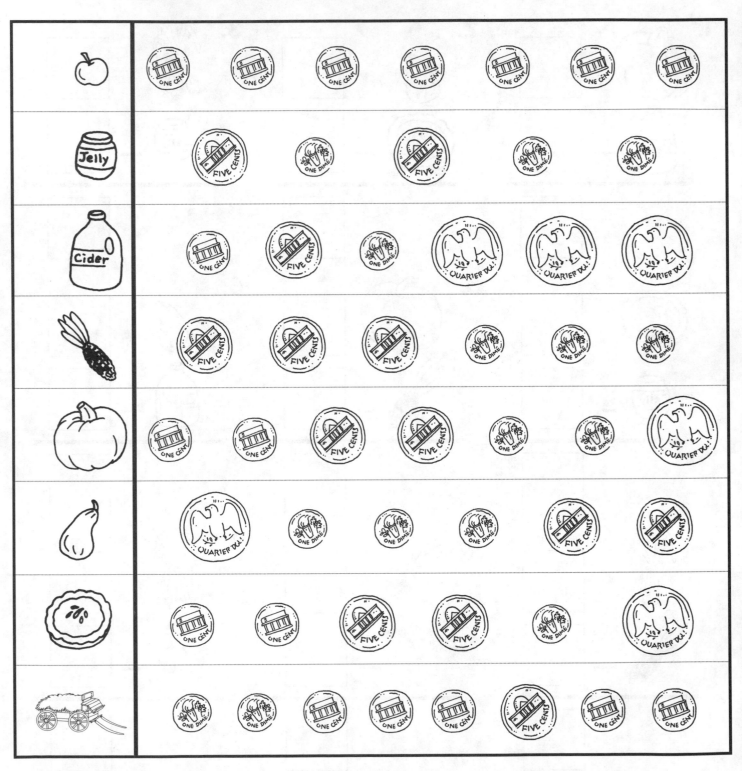

*Instant & Interactive Math Picture Pages With Activities*
Scholastic Professional Books

**Name:** _____

# Autumn Harvest Spending

What would you like to buy?

1. Use a red crayon. Circle what you will buy. Circle the coins you will need in red, too.

2. Use a blue crayon. Circle what you will buy next. Circle the coins you will need in blue, too.

3. Use a black crayon. Circle your third choice. Circle the coins you will need in black.

# Transportation

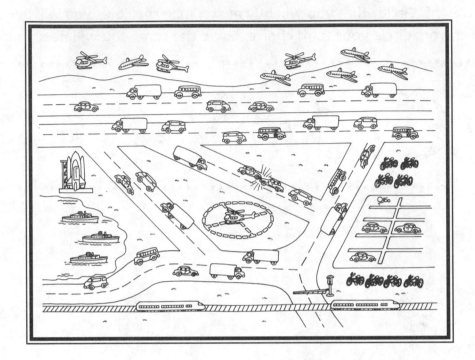

## Thoughts on the Theme

Most children love to travel and have enjoyed playing with toy vehicles. This transportation picture builds on children's interests while activating their math skills. You may want to introduce the word *vehicle* and discuss which vehicles children have ridden in. Also discuss the word for the operator of different types of vehicles—*driver, captain, pilot, astronaut, engineer,* or *rider.*

Make a copy of the Transportation theme picture for each child. Have children identify each vehicle. This picture provides an excellent opportunity to discuss safety rules for drivers and pedestrians.

## Using the Worksheets

Make copies of the worksheets that you want children to complete. Read the directions to the class and model how to do the first item.

- **Transportation Addition** requires children to count and then write the correct numbers to create the addition problems that they will solve. Point out that because children are adding unlike vehicles, they should express their answers as "vehicles."

- **Transportation Subtraction** also requires children to count and write the correct numbers to create the problems that they will solve. Since children are subtracting unlike vehi-

*Instant & Interactive Math Picture Pages With Activities*
Scholastic Professional Books

cles, they should express their answers as "more trucks than ships" or "vehicles."

❧ **Counting by Twos** provides practice in the skill of skip counting by twos. Remind children to assume that there are two people in each vehicle.

❧ For **Transportation Questions**, you may wish to read the questions aloud.

## More Math Ideas

**1.** Use the transportation picture for a measuring lesson. In inches or centimeters, have children measure the distance of the roads, the distance from one vehicle to another, or the distance that a vehicle would need to go from one point on the picture to another point.

**2.** Present a lesson on the concepts of > greater than, and < less than. For example, the number of cars is greater than the number of bicycles, because 10>8.

**3.** Give a money value to the cost of riding in each vehicle. Determine the type of coins or bills it would take to pay the fare. Add, subtract, or multiply the money values.

## Math and Writing

Use the math picture to generate writing ideas. For example, have children:

❧ Write a story about one of the vehicles and tell how far it travels and how fast it goes.

❧ Write additional subtraction problems about a bus that takes on and drops off people.

## Cross-Curriculum Bonus

*Music:* Teach children transportation songs such as: "I've Been Working on the Railroad," "The Wheels on the Bus Go 'Round and 'Round," or "Row, Row, Row Your Boat."

## Bookshelf Suggestions

❧ *Young Amelia Earhart* by Susan Alcott (Troll, 1992)

❧ *Clipper Ship* by Thomas P. Lewis (HarperCollins, 1992)

❧ *The Little Engine That Could* by Watty Piper (Grosset & Dunlap, 1978)

❧ *Grandfather's Journey* by Allen Say (Houghton Mifflin, 1993)

❧ *Young Orville and Wilbur Wright* by Andrew Woods (Troll, 1992)

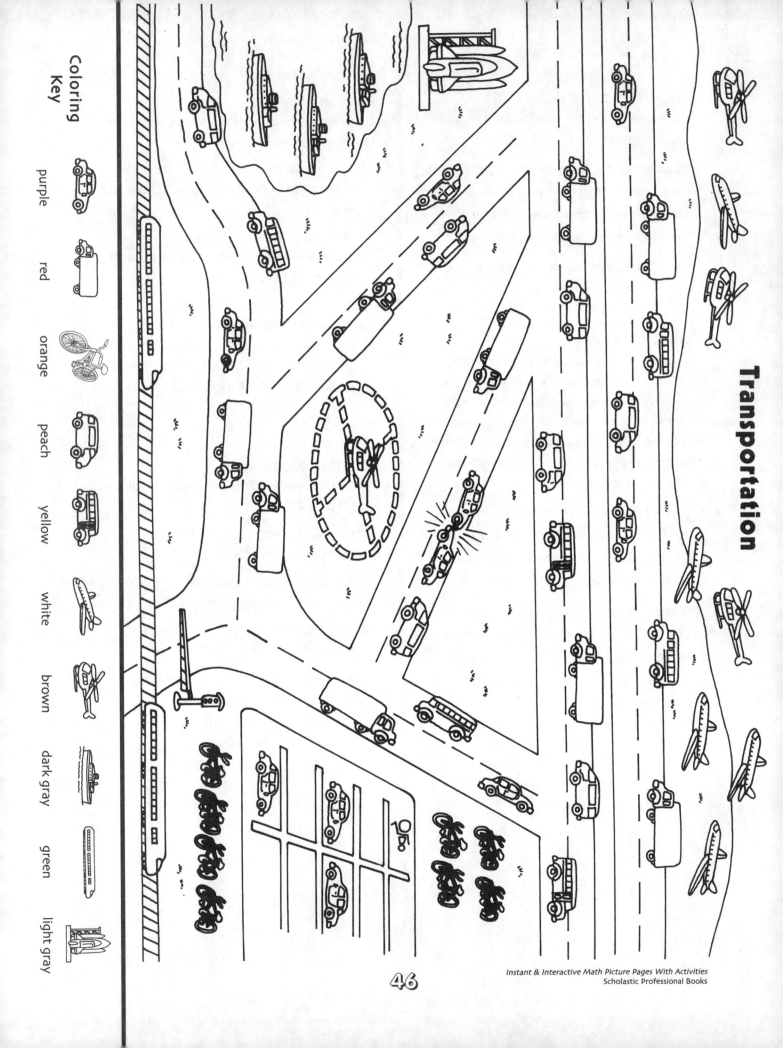

**Transportation**

*Instant & Interactive Math Picture Pages With Activities*
Scholastic Professional Books

# Transportation Addition

Use the math picture to count and write the number in each box. Add the numbers.

**1.**

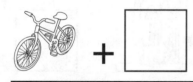 +

**2.**

 +

**3.**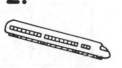

 +

**4.**

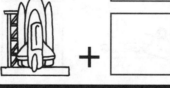 +

**5.**

 +

**6.**

 +

**7.**

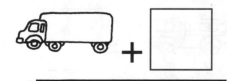 +

**8.**

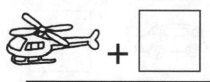 +

**9.**

*Instant & Interactive Math Picture Pages With Activities*
Scholastic Professional Books

# Transportation Subtraction

Use the math picture to count and write the number in each box. Subtract the numbers.

**1.** 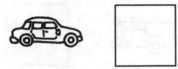 □

 — □

□

**2.**  □

 — □

□

**3.**  □

 — □

□

**4.**  □

 — □

□

**5.**  □

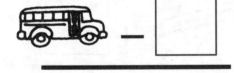 — □

□

**6.**  □

 — □

□

**7.** □

 — □

□

**8.** □

— □

□

**9.** □

— □

□

*Instant & Interactive Math Picture Pages With Activities*
Scholastic Professional Books

# Transportation Counting by Twos

Practice counting by twos: 2  4  6  8  10  12

Pretend that there are two people in or on each vehicle in the math picture.
Count by twos. Touch your fingertip to each vehicle as you count.
How many people are there all together for each type of vehicle? Write your answer
on the line beneath the vehicles pictured below.

**1.** _____        **2.** _____        **3.** _____

                    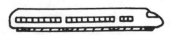

**4.** _____        **5.** _____        **6.** _____

Name: _____

# Transportation Questions

Use the math picture to answer the questions.

**1.** How many airplanes and helicopters are there all together?

_____

**2.** How many more cars are there than bicycles? _____

**3.** All the cars and vans want to park. How many parking spaces

are needed? _____

**4.** How many more airplanes are in the air than helicopters?

_____

**5.** There are 2 men in each truck. How many men are there in all?

_____

**6.** There are 5 children in each school bus. How many children are

riding buses in all? _____

**Challenge**

**7.** Each helicopter picks up 2 people on the way to the city and 5

people on the way back. How many people are picked up in

all? _____

*Instant & Interactive Math Picture Pages With Activities*
Scholastic Professional Books

# Holiday Toy Shop

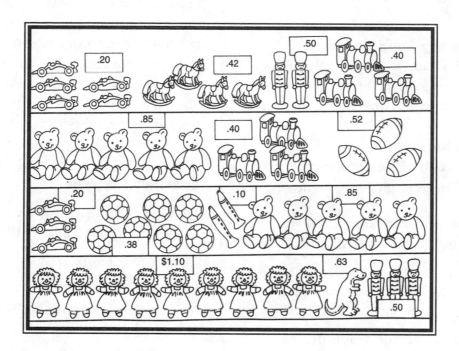

## Thoughts on the Theme

The month of December is a perfect time to teach about different holidays and traditions. Use the Holiday Toy Shop theme to weave math skills into your classroom discussions and celebrations. You'll find that this math picture is especially useful for teaching money skills; children will love buying the toys.

Make a copy of the Holiday Toy Shop picture for each child. Have children identify the toys and their prices.

## Using the Worksheets

Make copies of the worksheets that you want children to complete. Read the directions to the class and model how to do the first item.

◉ **Holiday Toy Shop Graphing** requires finding and counting each type of toy. Children then match that number to a numeral on the graph. Remind children to use a different color to make each bar of the graph.

◉ For **Holiday Toy Shop Addition**, have children count the number of each toy and then write that number in the box to create the addition problems that they will solve. Point out that because children are adding unlike toys, they should express their answers as "toys."

◉ **Holiday Toy Shop Subtraction** calls for children to identify and write the money value, write the price on the tag of the toy, and then subtract to determine the change. You may wish to have play money on hand for children to work with. Review how to write money using decimals.

◉ **Holiday Toy Shop Spending** requires children to count the money shown and look at the price tags to determine which toys they could buy.

## More Math Ideas

**1.** Use the math picture to generate word problems. For example, you might say:

◉ The store has nine dolls. If seven people buy dolls, how many dolls will be left?

◉ Can five boys each buy two balls? How do you know?

**2.** Write prices on the graph before duplicating it, and have children graph the prices.

**3.** Assign prices to the toys or use those on the math picture. Give children play money and ask which toys they would choose to buy with that amount of money. Change the amount of money each day.

**4.** Collect newspaper ads for toys and comparison shop.

## Math and Writing

Use the math picture to generate writing ideas. For example, have children:

◉ Write a story about buying one of the toys and tell how much money they had, how much they spent, and how much they had left over.

◉ Write an ad for a sale at the toy shop and include regular prices and sale prices.

## Cross-Curriculum Bonus

*Social Studies:* Teach about the different holiday customs celebrated by children in your class. Ask parents to come in to speak about their traditions and/or to cook traditional foods. Instead of your customary holiday party, plan a multicultural feast!

## Bookshelf Suggestions

◉ *Seven Candles for Kwanzaa* by Andrea Davis Pinkney (Puffin, 1998)

◉ *K Is for Kwanzaa* by Juwanda G. Ford (Cartwheel, 1997)

◉ *Christmas Around the World* by Emily Kelley (Lerner, 1976)

◉ *Arielle and the Hanukkah Surprise* by Devra Speregen and Shirley Newburger (Econo-Clad Books, 1999)

◉ *John Speirs' Happy Hanukkah* by Margery Gold (Golden Press, 1995)

*Instant & Interactive Math Picture Pages With Activities*
Scholastic Professional Books

# Holiday Toy Shop

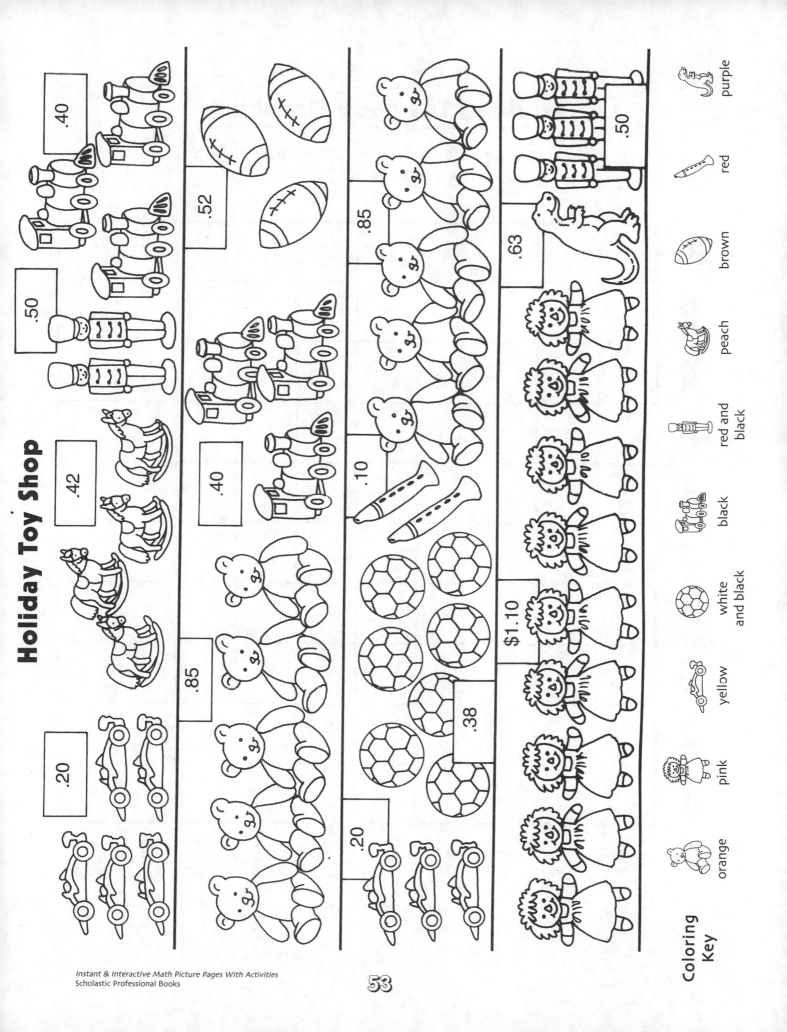

.40

.50

.42

.20

.52

.40

.85

.85

.10

.63

.50

.38

.20

$1.10

**Coloring Key**

| purple | red | brown | peach | red and black | black | white and black | yellow | pink | orange |

*Instant & Interactive Math Picture Pages With Activities*
Scholastic Professional Books

# Holiday Toy Shop Graphing

Use the math picture to count the number of each toy. Color the graph to show how many of each toy you count. Use a different color for each bar.

| 10 | | | | | | | | | | |
|----|--|--|--|--|--|--|--|--|--|--|
| 9 | | | | | | | | | | |
| 8 | | | | | | | | | | |
| 7 | | | | | | | | | | |
| 6 | | | | | | | | | | |
| 5 | | | | | | | | | | |
| 4 | | | | | | | | | | |
| 3 | | | | | | | | | | |
| 2 | | | | | | | | | | |
| 1 | | | | | | | | | | |

*Instant & Interactive Math Picture Pages With Activities*
Scholastic Professional Books

# Holiday Toy Shop Addition

Use the math picture to count and write the number in each box. Add the numbers.

**1.**
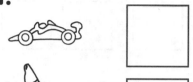

+

___

**2.**

+

___

**3.**

+

___

**4.**

+

___

**5.**

+

___

**6.**

+

___

**7.**
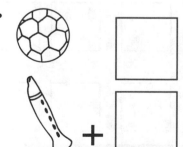

+

___

**8.**
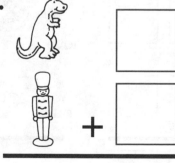

+

___

**9.**
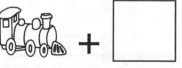

+

___

**Name:** _____

# Holiday Toy Shop Subtraction

Write the amount of money in the top box. Write the price in the box below. Subtract.

**1.**

You have:

$\square$ . $\square$ $\square$

You buy: — $\square$ . $\square$ $\square$

$\square$ . $\square$ $\square$

**2.**

You have:

$\square$ . $\square$ $\square$

You buy: — $\square$ . $\square$ $\square$

$\square$ . $\square$ $\square$

**3.**

You have:

$\square$ . $\square$ $\square$

You buy: — $\square$ . $\square$ $\square$

$\square$ . $\square$ $\square$

**4.**

You have:

$\square$ . $\square$ $\square$

You buy: — $\square$ . $\square$ $\square$

$\square$ . $\square$ $\square$

**5.**

You have:

$\square$ . $\square$ $\square$

You buy: — $\square$ . $\square$ $\square$

$\square$ . $\square$ $\square$

**6.**

You have:

$\square$ . $\square$ $\square$

You buy: — $\square$ . $\square$ $\square$

$\square$ . $\square$ $\square$

*Instant & Interactive Math Picture Pages With Activities*
Scholastic Professional Books

# Holiday Toy Shop Spending

What would you like to buy?

1. Use a red crayon. Circle what you will buy. Circle the coins you will need in green, too.

2. Use a blue crayon. Circle what you will buy next. Circle the coins you will need in blue, too.

3. Use a green crayon. Circle your third choice. Circle the coins you will need in green.

# The Food Pyramid

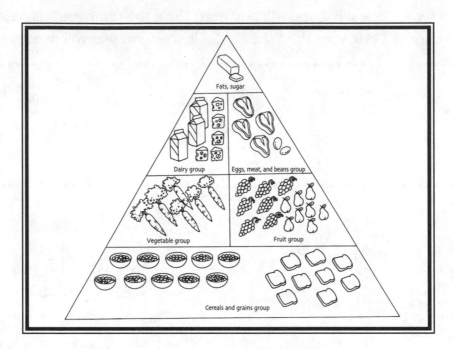

## Thoughts on the Theme
Teaching with the food pyramid coordinates well with studies about nutrition, as well as math.

Make a copy of the Food Pyramid theme picture for each child. Have children identify each food group. Discuss other foods not pictured that are in each food group. For example, pasta goes under cereals and grains, while chicken falls in the eggs, dried beans, and meat group.

## Using the Worksheets
Make copies of the worksheets that you want children to complete. Read the directions to the class and model how to do the first item.

- **Food Pyramid Addition** requires counting the number of each food and writing the number in the box. Children then add. Remind children to express their answers as "foods" since they are adding unlike foods.

- **Food Pyramid Subtraction** with money requires children to identify and write the value of the coins and bills and to write the price of the food. Children then subtract to determine the change. Review how to use decimal points correctly.

- For **Food Pyramid Multiplication**, children write the missing factor, then multiply. Remind children that they can check their answers by adding or counting.

*Instant & Interactive Math Picture Pages With Activities*
Scholastic Professional Books

For **Food Pyramid Questions**, children should write the name of a food on each blank line, then exchange papers with a classmate to solve the word problems.

## More Math Ideas

**1.** Use the math picture to generate more word problems. For example, you might say:

- How many sandwiches could you make with the bread that is pictured in the math picture?

- How many spoons are needed to eat the cereal in the picture?

**2.** Make a graph of favorite fruits or vegetables.

**3.** Ask children to bring in the food advertisement section from the newspaper. Cut out two or three food items for breakfast and add the cost. Do the same for lunch, dinner, and snacks.

**4.** Provide children with an additional food pyramid, and ask them to make a tally mark in the correct food group for each food that they eat for one day. Be sure to tell them that many foods will be a combination of several food groups, and they need to make a mark for each group.

## Math and Writing

Use the math picture to generate writing ideas. For example, have children:

- Take surveys and make tallies of three kinds of food classmates eat at lunch. Children can then write a summary of the tally results.

- Write recipes for making a favorite sandwich.

## Cross-Curriculum Bonus

*Social Studies:* Set up a restaurant in your classroom. Make menus and have some children order food while their classmates are the waiters/waitresses, who add the bill and collect play money as payment. Diners should also leave a tip. A 10 percent tip is easy; tell children to drop the last numeral. After practicing 10 percent, students can graduate to becoming more generous tippers and doubling the tip to be 20 percent. Use either plastic food or pictures of food cut from food boxes and containers or magazines. Other social skills, such as manners, table setting, and role-playing restaurant jobs are a natural part of your classroom restaurant.

## Bookshelf Suggestions

- *Cloudy With A Chance of Meatballs* by Judi Barrett (Aladdin, 1982)

- *The Wolf's Chicken Stew* by Keiko Kasza (Paper Star, 1996)

- *The Giant Jam Sandwich* by John Vernon Lord (Houghton Mifflin, 1987)

- *Stone Soup* by Ann McGovern (Scholastic, 1987)

- *Gregory, the Terrible Eater* by Mitchell Sharmat (Scholastic, 1989)

# The Food Pyramid

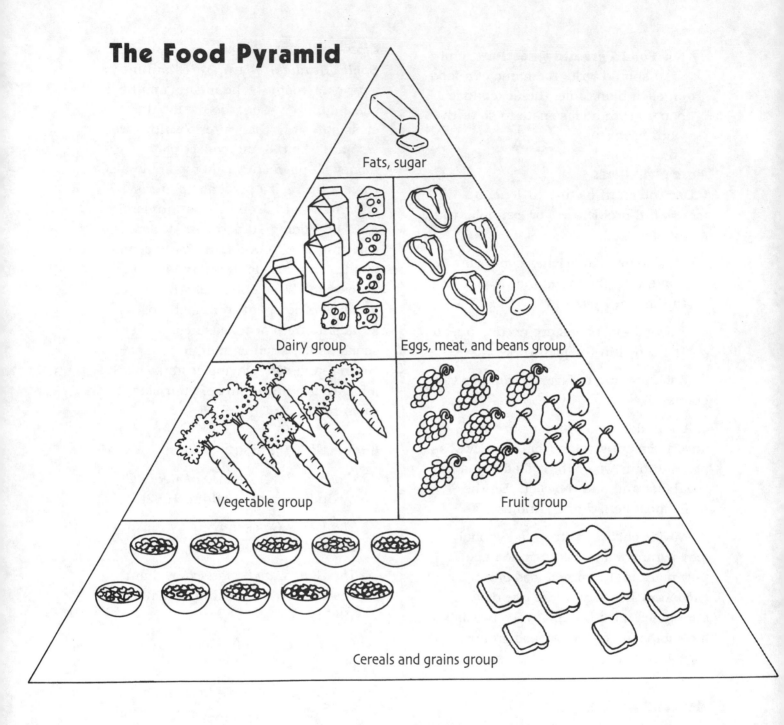

Fats, sugar

Dairy group

Eggs, meat, and beans group

Vegetable group

Fruit group

Cereals and grains group

## Coloring and Pricing Key

red
$1.10

brown
.95

light green
.85

purple
.80

orange
.75

peach
.50

pink
.60

blue
.45

white
.65

yellow
.40

*Instant & Interactive Math Picture Pages With Activities*
Scholastic Professional Books

**Name:** _____

# Food Pyramid Addition

Count one type of food from the food group noted. Then, count one type of food from the other food group noted. Add the combination of foods together.

**1.**
Dairy

Vegetable +

_____

**2.**
Fruit

Fats, sugar +

_____

**3.**
Cereals and grains

Dairy +

_____

**4.**
Eggs, meat, and beans

Fruit +

_____

**5.**
Vegetable

Cereals and grains +

_____

**6.**
Fats, sugar

Dairy +

_____

**7.**
Vegetable

Fruit +

_____

**8.**
Fats, sugar

Eggs, meat, and beans +

_____

**9.**
Cereals and grains

Fruit +

_____

Instant & Interactive Math Picture Pages With Activities
Scholastic Professional Books

# Food Pyramid Subtraction With Money

Write the amount of money in the top box. Write the price in the box below. Subtract.

**1.**
You have:

⬜ . ⬜ ⬜

You buy:

— ⬜ . ⬜ ⬜

⬜ . ⬜ ⬜

**2.**
You have:

⬜ . ⬜ ⬜

You buy:

— ⬜ . ⬜ ⬜

⬜ . ⬜ ⬜

**3.**
You have:

⬜ . ⬜ ⬜

You buy:

— ⬜ . ⬜ ⬜

⬜ . ⬜ ⬜

**4.**
You have:

⬜ . ⬜ ⬜

You buy:

— ⬜ . ⬜ ⬜

⬜ . ⬜ ⬜

**5.**
You have:

⬜ . ⬜ ⬜

You buy:

— ⬜ . ⬜ ⬜

⬜ . ⬜ ⬜

**6.**
You have:

⬜ . ⬜ ⬜

You buy:

— ⬜ . ⬜ ⬜

⬜ . ⬜ ⬜

Instant & Interactive Math Picture Pages With Activities
Scholastic Professional Books

# Food Pyramid Multiplication

Count the food items pictured. Multiply the numbers

**1.**
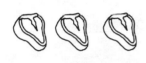

3 x ☐ = ☐

**2.**

2 x ☐ = ☐

**3.**

4 x ☐ = ☐

**4.**

3 x ☐ = ☐

**5.**

2 x ☐ = ☐

**6.**

2 x ☐ = ☐

**7.**

3 x ☐ = ☐

**8.**

3 x ☐ = ☐

**9.**

5 x ☐ = ☐

# Food Pyramid Questions

Write the name of a food from the math picture on each blank line. Change papers with a classmate. Solve each other's problems.

**1.** How many _____ and _____ are there in all? _____

**2.** How many fewer _____ are there than _____? _____

**3.** Gail crosses out two _____. How many are left? _____

**4.** How many _____ and _____ and _____ are there in all? _____

**5.** Dad draws three more _____ on the math picture. How many are there now? _____

**6.** Mom draws eight bagels in the cereals and grains group. How many pictures are there in that group now? _____

**7.** Write a word problem of your own.

_____

_____

_____

_____

_____

_____

*Instant & Interactive Math Picture Pages With Activities*
Scholastic Professional Books

# Snow Sports

## Thoughts on the Theme

Children will enjoy visiting the slopes of the Snow Sports math picture in the winter or at any time of the year.

Make a copy of the Snow Sports theme picture for each child. Have children identify the animals and winter sports equipment in the picture. Be sure to point out to children that the skis, ski poles, snowshoes, and skates are all counted separately, not as pairs - ten skis, nine ski poles, six snowshoes, and eight skates.

## Using the Worksheets

Make copies of the worksheets that you want children to complete. Read the directions to the class and model how to do the first item.

**Snow Sports Addition** calls for children to count and then write the correct numbers to create the addition problems that they will solve. On this page, children will be adding three numbers. Point out that because children are adding unlike things, they should express their answers as "animals" or "winter sports items."

**Snow Sports Subtraction** also requires children to count and write the correct numbers to create the problems that they will solve. Since children are subtracting unlike things, they should express their answers as "more skis than sleds" or "winter items."

- For the **Snow Sports Multiplication** worksheet, explain that children should count how many there are of each animal or item. Then, they should write that number in each box and multiply.

- **Snow Sports Questions** call for children to read the questions, and count the number of animals and items in the math picture to solve the problems.

## More Math Ideas

**1.** Use the Snow Sports picture for a measuring lesson. Using inches or centimeters, have children measure the length and width of the ice rink, the distance from one moose to another moose, or the distance that a sled, toboggan, or skier would need to go from one point on the picture to another point.

**2.** Present a lesson on the concepts of > greater than, and < less than. For example, the number of skis is greater than the number of ski poles, because 10>9.

**3.** Have your own Winter Olympics on either a snowy playground or a sunny blacktop. Involve children in measuring skills—how far, how fast, how high, and so on. Keep records to make comparisons.

**4.** Have children fold paper to cut out snowflakes, then conduct a lesson on symmetry.

## Math and Writing

Use the math picture to generate writing ideas. For example, have children:

- Write a story about a moose skater who not only can make figure eights in the ice, but other geometric shapes as well.

- Write dialogue for the animals in the picture.

- Write about the problem caused by having ten skis and only nine ski poles. Offer a solution!

## Cross-Curriculum Bonus

*Science:* Experiment with ice. How can you melt it faster? What materials can you use to insulate it so that it melts slower?

## Bookshelf Suggestions

- *Katy and the Big Snow* by Virginia Lee Burton (Sandpiper, 1974)

- *Stopping by the Woods on a Snowy Evening* by Robert Frost (Dutton, 1985)

- *The Snowy Day* by Ezra Jack Keats (Viking Press, 1981)

- *Nate the Great and the Snowy Trail* by Marjorie Weinman Sharmat (Young Yearling, 1984)

- *Mitten: An Old Ukranian Folktale* by Alvin R. Tresselt (Turtleback Books, 1989)

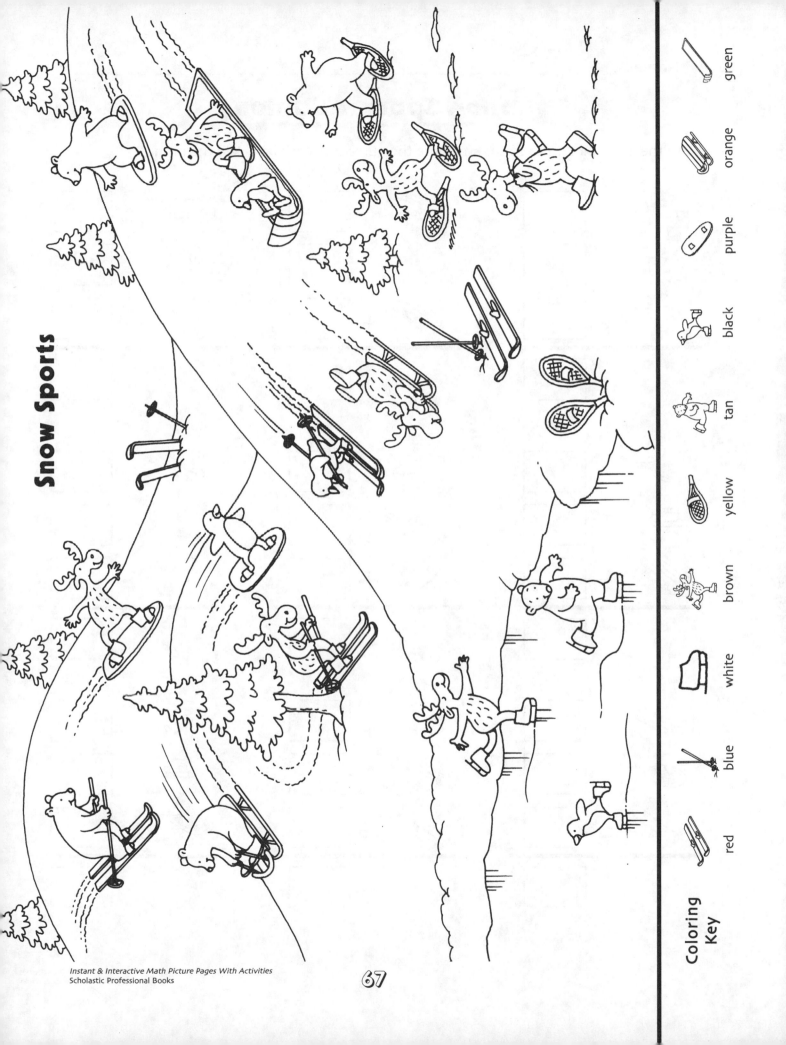

# Snow Sports

green

orange

purple

black

tan

yellow

brown

white

blue

red

**Coloring Key**

Instant & Interactive Math Picture Pages With Activities
Scholastic Professional Books

# Snow Sports Addition

Use the math picture to count and write the number in each box. Add the numbers.

**1.**

+

**2.**
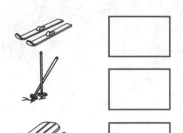

+

**3.**
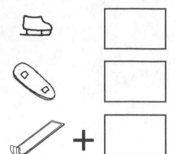

+

**4.**
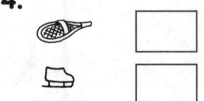

+

**5.**
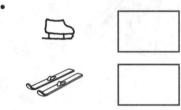

+

**6.**
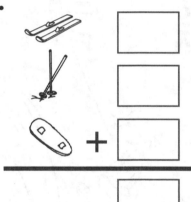

+

**7.**
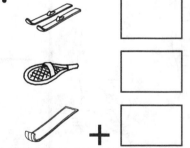

+

**8.**
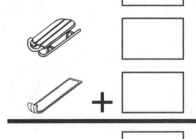

+

**9.**
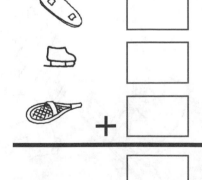

+

*Instant & Interactive Math Picture Pages With Activities*
Scholastic Professional Books

# Snow Sports Subtraction

Use the math picture to count and write the number in each box. Subtract the numbers.

**1.**

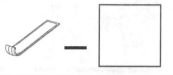
☐
−☐
_____
☐

**2.**

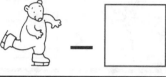
☐
−☐
_____
☐

**3.**

☐
−☐
_____
☐

**4.**

☐
−☐
_____
☐

**5.**

☐
−☐
_____
☐

**6.**

☐
−☐
_____
☐

**7.**
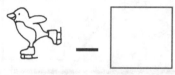
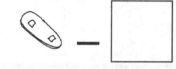
☐
−☐
_____
☐

**8.**

☐
−☐
_____
☐

**9.**

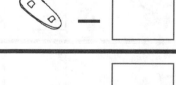
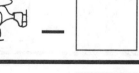
☐
−☐
_____
☐

Name: _____

# Snow Sports Multiplication

Count the number of animals and items in the math picture. Write that number in each box. Multiply.

**1.**
  ☐

X ☐
_____

☐

**2.**   ☐

X ☐
_____

☐

**3.**   ☐

X ☐
_____

☐

**4.**   ☐

X ☐
_____

☐

**5.**   ☐

X ☐
_____

☐

**6.**   ☐

X ☐
_____

☐

**7.**   ☐
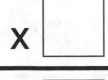

X ☐
_____

☐

**8.**   ☐
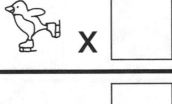

X ☐
_____

☐

**9.**   ☐

X ☐
_____

☐

*Instant & Interactive Math Picture Pages With Activities*
Scholastic Professional Books

# Snow Sports Questions

Use the math picture to answer the questions.

**1.** How many bears, moose, and penguins are there all together?

_____ animals

**2.** How many more skis are there than ski poles?     _____ ski(s)

**3.** How many animals are sledding and skating in all?

_____ animals

**4.** If each penguin has a pair of mittens, how many mittens are

there in all? _____ mittens

**5.** The skaters are not wearing boots.  Many other animals are

wearing a pair of boots.  How many boots are there in all?

_____ boots

**6.** How many more ice skates are there than snowboards?

_____ ice skates

**7.** How many more animals are on the snow than on the ice?

_____ animals on the snow

# Dinomathic Park

## Thoughts on the Theme

Welcome your children to Dinomathic Park, a great way to learn about dinosaurs while doing math. Explain that this math picture is just a collection of favorite dinosaurs. These dinosaurs did not all live in the same period of time or in the same geographic location.

Make a copy of the Dinomathic Park theme picture for each child. Introduce each dinosaur: *Coelophysis, Stegosaurus, Ankylosaurus, Triceratops, Trachodon, Tyrannosaurus Rex, Acrocanthosaurus, Corythosaurus, Brachiosaurus*, and *Elasimosaurus*. The math picture offers an opportunity to discuss the time periods - *Triassic, Jurassic*, and *Cretaceous*; the features of the dinosaurs; which ones were plant eaters and which ones were meat eaters.

## Using the Worksheets

Make copies of the worksheets that you want children to complete. Read the directions to the class and model how to do the first item.

- **Dinomathic Park Addition** requires students to count and then write the correct numbers to create the addition problems that they will solve. Children will be adding three numbers. Point out that children should express their answers as "dinosaurs."

- **Dinomathic Park Measuring** asks children to find the two dinosaurs of each kind that are farthest apart and measure the distance. Children will need to cut out the ruler first. Note that children can measure in both inches and centimeters.

*Instant & Interactive Math Picture Pages With Activities*
Scholastic Professional Books

⊚ The **Dinomathic Park Addition, Multiplication, & Division** page provides children with a visual representation of the relationship between addition and multiplication. For example, for Stegosaurus, children can see that three sets of three Stegosauruses is 3+3+3=9 or 3 X 3=9. Extend the activity by having children write division problems: 9 divided by 3=3. However, if you're using page 77 as an introductory division lesson, consider doing the page as a whole class activity.

⊚ **Dinomathic Park Questions** require children to read the questions and count the number of dinosaurs to write the equation to be solved. Children should be reminded to label their answers with the word "dinosaurs" after the number.

## More Math Ideas

**1.** The three periods of time in the Mesozoic Era provide a great opportunity to discuss place value and how to separate hundreds, thousands and millions with commas. The Mesozoic Era was 225,000,000 years to 65,000,000 years ago. The Triassic period was from 225,000,000 years to 180,000,000 years ago. The Jurassic period was from 180,000,000 to 130,000,000 years ago and the Cretaceous period lasted from about 130,000,000 to 65,000,000 years ago.

**2.** The topic of dinosaurs provides an opportunity for using math to make scaled drawings. Using one inch to equal one foot, or in the case of very large dinosaurs, using one inch to equal ten feet, children will enjoy using math to draw their favorite dinosaur.

**3.** Graph the number of each type of dinosaur in the picture. Also make a graph of which type of dinosaur is the favorite in your classroom, or survey several classrooms to make a graph.

## Math and Writing

Use the math picture to generate writing ideas. For example, have children:

⊚ Write "baseball card" statistics for each dinosaur.

⊚ Write an invitation to Dinomathic Park including its address, the time to come, how long the visit should be, and the numbers of dinosaurs who will greet guests.

## Cross-Curriculum Bonus

*Language Arts:* Make a list of new vocabulary words. In addition to the names of dinosaurs, include words such as *Mesozoic, Triassic, Jurassic, Cretaceous, era, archeologist,* and *paleontologist.* Have students alphabetize the list.

## Bookshelf Suggestions

⊚ *Dinosaur Bones* by Aliki (HarperTrophy, 1990)

⊚ *Patrick's Dinosaur and Big Old Bones* by Carol Carrick (Clarion, 1992)

⊚ *Danny and the Dinosaur* by Syd Hoff (HarperTrophy, 1993)

⊚ *Dinosaur Bob* by William Joyce (HarperCollins, 1998)

⊚ *Dinosaur Time* by Peggy Parish (HarperTrophy, 1983)

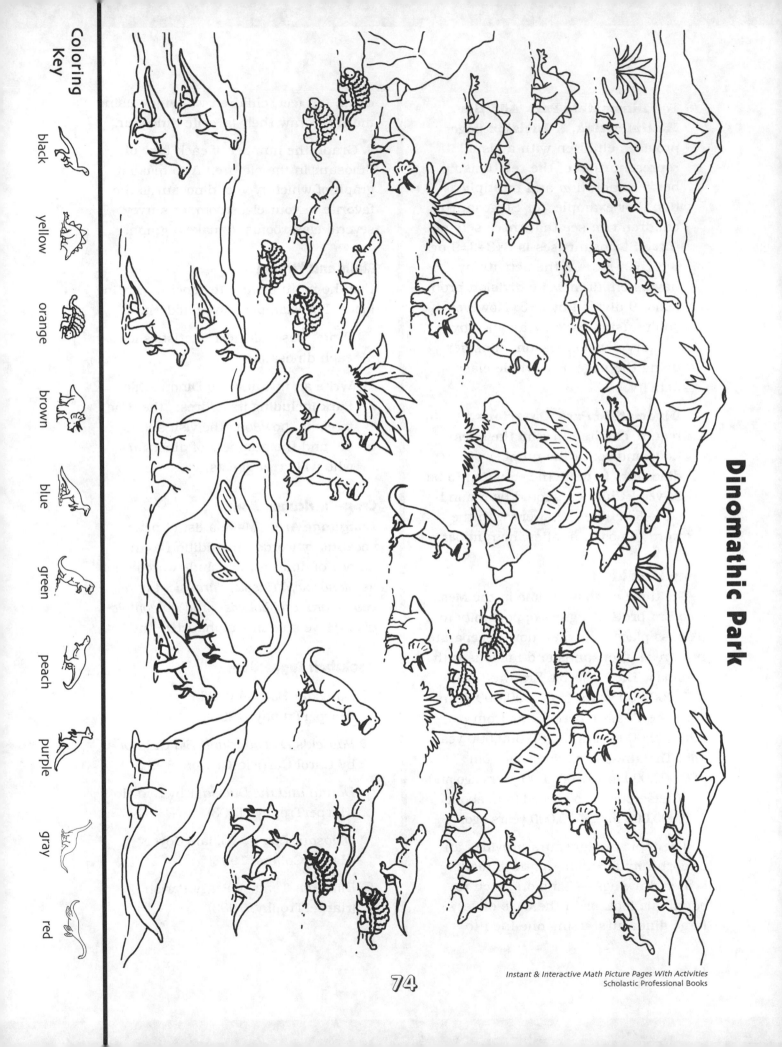

## Coloring Key

black
yellow
orange
brown
blue
green
peach
purple
gray
red

# Dinomathic Park

# Dinomathic Park Addition

Use the math picture to count and write the number in each box. Add the numbers.

**1.**    +

**2.**    +

**3.**    +

**4.**   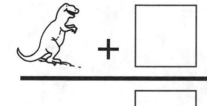 +

**5.**  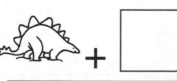 +

**6.** 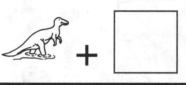  +

**Name:** _____

# Dinomathic Park Measuring

Cut out the ruler. Use the math picture. Find the two dinosaurs of each kind that are farthest apart. Measure the distance between them, from head to head. Then, round to the nearest centimeter.

1.  _____

2.  _____

3.  _____

4.  _____

5.  _____

6.  _____

7.  _____

8.  _____

9. 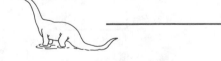 _____

*Instant & Interactive Math Picture Pages With Activities*
Scholastic Professional Books

Name: _____

# Dinomathic Park Addition, Multiplication & Division

Write an addition problem, a multiplication problem, and a division problem.

**1.** Find the two groups of  on the math picture.

$+$ ☐ ☐   $-$ ☐ ☐   ☐ ⟌☐

**2.** Look at the groups of  on the math picture.

$+$ ☐ ☐   $-$ ☐ ☐   ☐ ⟌☐

**3.** Look at the groups of  on the math picture.

$+$ ☐ ☐   $-$ ☐ ☐   ☐ ⟌☐

**4.** Look at the groups of 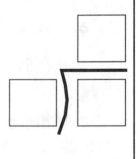 on the math picture.

$+$ ☐ ☐   $-$ ☐ ☐   ☐ ⟌☐

**Name:** _____

# Dinomathic Park Questions

Use the math picture to answer these questions.

**1.** If each [dinosaur] eats ten insects a day, how many insects will be

eaten today? _____ insects

**2.** How many more [Triceratops] are there than [T-rex] ? _____ Triceratops

**3.** Each [Triceratops] eats five plants a day.  How many plants are eaten

in one day? _____ plants

**4.** Every [Stegosaurus] in the park weighs two tons.

How much do they weigh in all? _____ tons

**5.** How many [Stegosaurus] and [Triceratops] are there all together?

_____ in all

**6.** Two of the [Ankylosaurus] are leaving the park.  How many [Ankylosaurus] will be

left in the park? _____ Ankylosaurus

**7.** Write a word problem of your own.

_____

_____

*Instant & Interactive Math Picture Pages With Activities*
Scholastic Professional Books

# Insects
## (Crawling With Math)

### Thoughts on the Theme

Most children love to observe insects, and even those who are squeamish about them will be able to satisfy some of their curiosity with this math picture.

Make a copy of the Insect theme picture for each child. Introduce each insect: *grasshopper, luna moth, bee, praying mantis, ladybug, house fly, monarch butterfly, firefly, water beetle, ant.* The math picture offers an opportunity to discuss the different features of each insect.

### Using the Worksheets

Make copies of the worksheets that you want children to complete. Read the directions to the class and model how to do the first item.

- **Insect Addition** asks students to count and then write the correct numbers to create the addition problems that they will solve. Point out that children should express their answers as "insects."

- **Measuring Insects** requires children to find the two insects of each kind that are farthest apart and measure the distance between them. In some cases, children will have to estimate this distance before measuring. Have children cut out the ruler before beginning. Note that they can measure in inches and centimeters.

**Insect Symmetry** calls for children to identify the correct half to make a symmetrical insect. For item 6, children must draw the other half. You may wish to follow up this page by having children find examples of other things that are symmetrical.

For **Insect Questions**, children read the questions and count the number of insects to write the equation to be solved. Note that children are asked to estimate and then count for question 7.

## More Math Ideas

**1.** The topic of insects provides an opportunity for using math to make scaled drawings. Using the sizes of the insects in the math picture, measure each insect and draw them four times as large. You may want to do this math as a whole class project.

**2.** Graph the number of each type of insect in the picture. Also make a graph of which type of insect is the favorite in your classroom, or survey several classrooms to make a graph.

## Math and Writing

Use the math picture to generate writing ideas. For example, have children:

Write an insect counting song using traditional words. Example:
Ten little ants come out to play.
Oh, those ants have fun today!

Write directions to locate a specific insect in the math picture. Encourage the use of direction words such as "left" and "right."

## Cross-Curriculum Bonus

*Art:* Children might make insects from scrap materials such as egg cartons, pipe cleaners, gauze, rocks, felt, clay, toothpicks, and tissue paper. Have children label their insects and write a descriptive sentence about them. Display them in the classroom or a school showcase.

## Bookshelf Suggestions

*The Very Quiet Cricket* by Eric Carle (Putnam, 1997)

*Where Butterflies Grow* by Joanne Ryder (Puffin Books, 1996)

*The Icky Bug Alphabet Book* by Jerry Pallotta (Charlesbridge, 1990)

*Bugs* by Nancy Winslow Parker and Joan Richards Wright (William Morrow & Co., 1988)

*Two Bad Ants* by Chris Van Allsburg (Houghton Mifflin, 1988)

*Instant & Interactive Math Picture Pages With Activities*
Scholastic Professional Books

**Insects - Crawling With Math**

*Instant & Interactive Math Picture Pages With Activities*
Scholastic Professional Books

**Coloring Key**

| | |
|---|---|
| green | |
| light green | |
| yellow and black | |
| peach | |
| red | |
| dark gray | |
| orange | |
| yellow | |
| brown | |
| black | |

# Insect Addition

Use the math picture to count and write the number for each box. Add the numbers.

**1.**

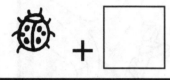  +

_____

**2.**

  +

_____

**3.**

+

_____

**4.**
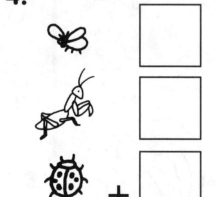

+

_____

**5.**
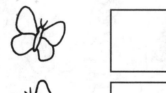

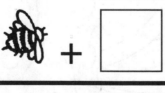  +

_____

**6.**

  +

_____

Instant & Interactive Math Picture Pages With Activities
Scholastic Professional Books

# Measuring Insects

Cut out the ruler. Use the math picture. Find the two insects of each kind that are farthest apart. Measure the distance between them, from head to head. Then, round to the nearest centimeter.

1.  _____

2.  _____

3.  _____

4.  _____

5.  _____

6.  _____

**Name:** _____

# Insect Symmetry

Both sides of an insect are alike. Look at the picture on the left. Circle the picture on the right that shows the rest of the insect.

**1.**

**2.**

**3.**

**4.**

**5.**

**6.** Draw the
other half of
the butterfly.

*Instant & Interactive Math Picture Pages With Activities*
Scholastic Professional Books

# Insect Questions

Use the math picture to answer the questions.

**1.** How many moths and butterflies are there in all? _____ insects

**2.** How many more ants are there than ladybugs? _____ ants

**3.** If the fireflies, bees, and house flies all fly away, how many insects will fly away? _____ insects

**4.** Each ladybug has ten spots. How many spots is that in all? _____ spots

**5.** The water beetles each have two antennas. How many antennas are there all together? Count by twos. _____ antennas

**6.** If the ants go marching two by two, how many pairs of ants are marching? _____ pairs

**7.** Estimate how many flying insects are in the picture - flies, bees, luna moths, monarch butterflies, fireflies, and ladybugs. Estimate _____ Count to check your guess. Count _____

# Pleasant Pond Park

## Thoughts on the Theme

Take children on a trip to Pleasant Pond Park and add a little sunshine to their math lesson.

Make a copy of the Pleasant Pond Park theme picture for each child. Note that the picture offers an opportunity to discuss swimming and playground safety.

## Using the Worksheets

Make copies of the worksheets that you want children to complete. Read the directions to the class and model how to do the first item.

### ✐ Pleasant Pond Park Addition

requires children to count and then write the correct numbers to create the addition problems that they will solve. Point out that because children are adding unlike animals or objects, they should express their answers as "animals," "carousel animals," or "Pleasant Pond Park items."

### ✐ Pleasant Pond Park Subtraction

also asks children to count and write the correct numbers to create the problems that they will solve. Since children are subtracting unlike animals or objects, they should express their answers as "more frogs than ducks" or "Pleasant Pond Park items."

### ✐ Pleasant Pond Park Measuring

calls for children to find what is to be measured in the picture and to

Instant & Interactive Math Picture Pages With Activities
Scholastic Professional Books

measure in either inches or centimeters. Have children cut out the ruler before they begin.

@ For **Pleasant Pond Park Questions**, children read the questions and use the math picture to solve the problems.

## More Math Ideas

**1.** Graph the number of each item in the picture. Also make a graph of which type of amusement is the favorite in your classroom, or survey several classrooms to make a graph.

**2.** Assign other money values to the amusements in the picture, and discuss which coins or bills would be needed to pay for each.

## Math and Writing

Use the math picture to generate writing ideas. For example, have children:

@ Write a newspaper article giving facts about things to do at Pleasant Pond Park. Suggest that children include the number of rides and rentals.

@ Select a duck or frog from the math picture. Tell about their adventures at Pleasant Pond Park. Include: how many rides the animal takes, how much money it spends, and other information.

## Cross-Curriculum Bonus

*Science:* Conduct experiments to see which classroom objects sink or float. Have children write predictions for each item beforehand. Try using: a bar of soap, paperclip, sponge, toy sailboat, penny, piece of paper, leaf, pencil. Check children's predictions against the results.

## Bookshelf Suggestions

@ *Frog and Toad are Friends* by Arnold Lobel (HarperCollins, 1979)

@ *Make Way for Ducklings* by Robert McCloskey (Puffin, 1999)

@ *The Frog Alphabet Book* by Jerry Pallotta (Charlesbridge, 1990)

@ *Farmer Duck* by Martin Waddell (Candlewick Press, 1996)

@ *Red-Eyed Tree Frog* by Joy Cowley (Scholastic, 1999)

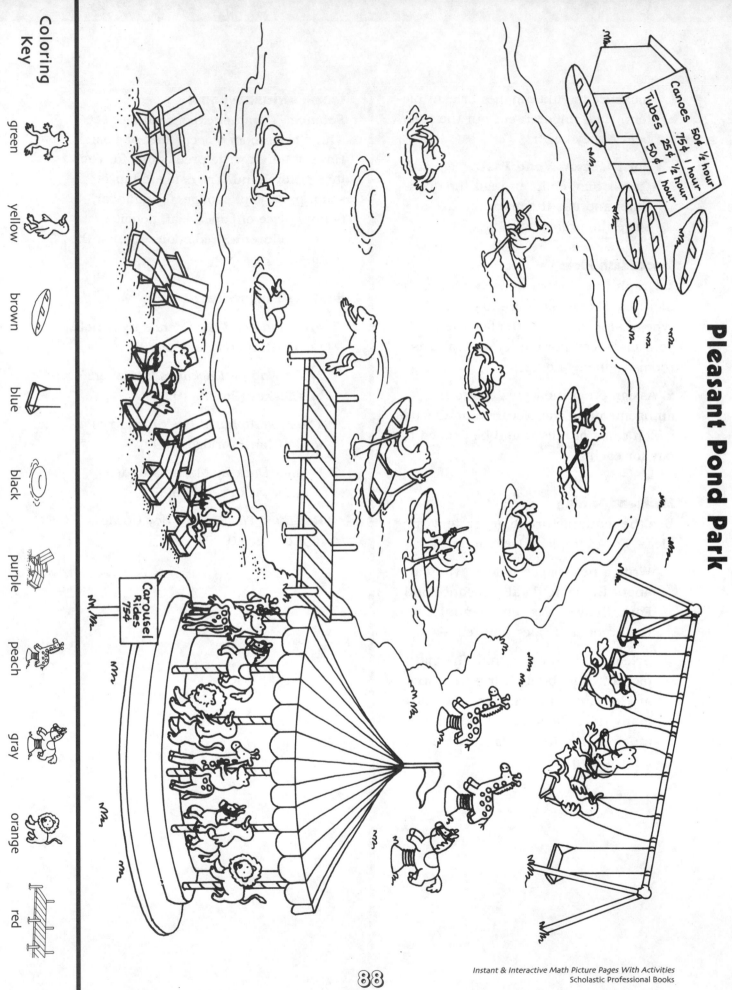

**Pleasant Pond Park**

Canoes 50¢ ½ hour
75¢ 1 hour
Tubes 25¢ ½ hour
50¢ 1 hour

Carousel Rides 75¢

**Coloring Key**

green
yellow
brown
blue
black
purple
peach
gray
orange
red

*Instant & Interactive Math Picture Pages With Activities*
Scholastic Professional Books

**Name:** _____

# Pleasant Pond Park Addition

Use the math picture to count and write the number in each box. Add the numbers.

**1.**

☐
☐
+

————————

☐

**2.**

☐
☐
+

————————

☐

**3.**

☐
☐
+

————————

☐

**4.**
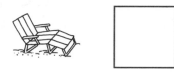

☐
☐
+

————————

☐

**5.**

☐
☐
+

————————

☐

**6.**

☐
☐
+

————————

☐

**7.**
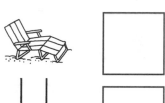

☐
☐
+

————————

☐

**8.**

☐
☐
+

————————

☐

**9.**

☐
☐
+

————————

☐

Name: _____

# Pleasant Pond Park Subtraction

Use the math picture to count and write the number in each box. Subtract the numbers.

**1.**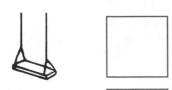
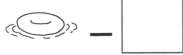
 — ☐
☐
_____
☐

**2.**
  ☐
— ☐
_____
☐

**3.**
☐
☐
— ☐
_____
☐

**4.**  ☐
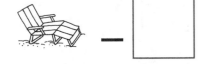 — ☐
_____
☐

**5.**  ☐
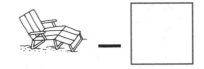 — ☐
_____
☐

**6.**  ☐
 — ☐
_____
☐

**7.**  ☐
 — ☐
_____
☐

**8.**  ☐
 — ☐
_____
☐

**9.**  ☐
   — ☐
_____
☐

Instant & Interactive Math Picture Pages With Activities
Scholastic Professional Books

**Name:** _____

# Pleasant Pond Park Measuring

Use the math picture. Measure to get the answers. Round to the nearest centimeter.

**1.** Measure how long the pond is. Measure how wide it is.

How long _____ How wide _____

**2.** How far from each other are the two frogs in tubes?

_____

**3.** Measure how long the dock is. Measure how wide it is.

How long _____ How wide _____

**4.** How far is the empty tube from the dock? _____

**5.** How far is the floating duck from the dock? _____

**6.** How far away from each other are the two ducks in the tubes? _____

**7.** Measure how tall the swing set is. Measure how wide it is.

How tall _____ How wide _____

# Pleasant Pond Park Questions

Use the math picture to answer the questions.

**1.** If a beach chair rental is .25 an hour, and all of the beach chairs were used for one hour, how much money was made? _____

**2.** There are seven swings. All the ducks want to swing at once. How many ducks have to wait a turn? _____ ducks

**3.** A duck has $3.00. He rides on the carousel two times. How much does he spend? _____ How much does he have left over? _____ Can he rent a canoe for half an hour? _____

**4.** There are eight canoes. They are all rented for half an hour. How much money is made? _____

**5.** All the frogs are going to have a canoe race. Two frogs fit into a canoe. How many canoes will the frogs need? _____ canoes How much will the race cost for half an hour? _____

**6.** How many tubes are in the water? _____ tubes. If each tube is rented for half an hour, how much money is made? _____

**7.** If you rode on the carousel once, rented a canoe for a half hour, and rented a tube for a half hour, how much would it cost?

_____

*Instant & Interactive Math Picture Pages With Activities*
Scholastic Professional Books

**Name:** _____

# Reproducible Mini-Characters

Copy these mini-characters onto the blank reproducible worksheets on pages 95–100 to create your own worksheets. You can also have children make up pages for their class-mates to do.

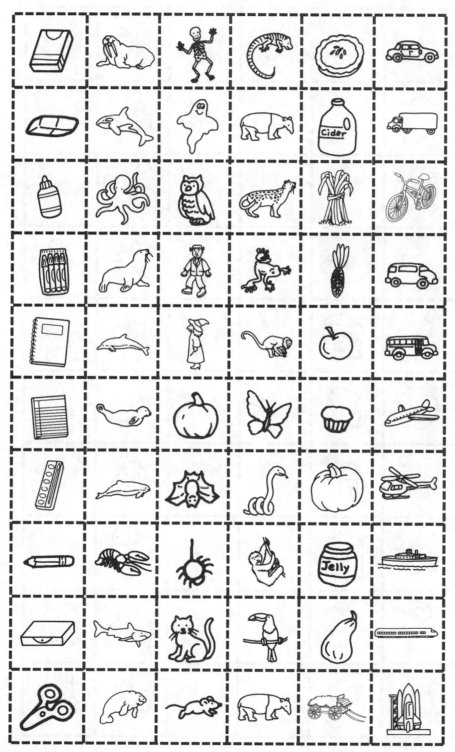

**Name:** _____

# Reproducible Mini-Characters

Copy these mini-characters onto the blank reproducible worksheets on pages 95–100 to create your own worksheets. You can also have children make up pages for their class-mates to do.

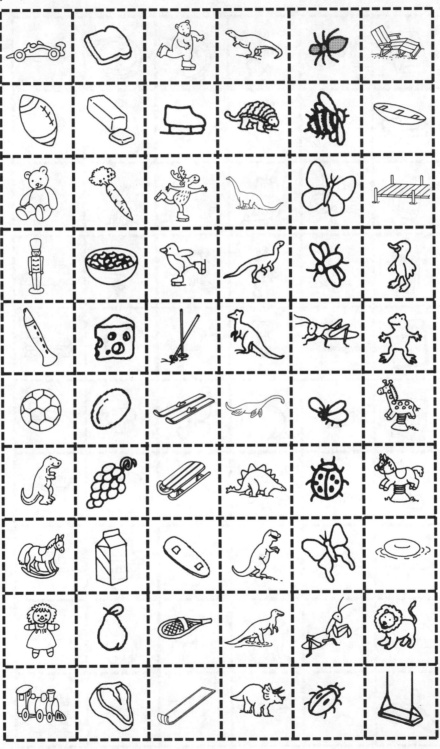

# Counting

Count each thing on the math picture. Trace that number with a crayon. Be sure to start at the top of the number. Then, take your pencil and trace the other numbers in the row.

1. [paste picture here] 1 2 3 4 5 6 7 8 9 10

2. [paste picture here] 1 2 3 4 5 6 7 8 9 10

3. [paste picture here] 1 2 3 4 5 6 7 8 9 10

4. [paste picture here] 1 2 3 4 5 6 7 8 9 10

5. [paste picture here] 1 2 3 4 5 6 7 8 9 10

6. [paste picture here] 1 2 3 4 5 6 7 8 9 10

7. [paste picture here] 1 2 3 4 5 6 7 8 9 10

8. [paste picture here] 1 2 3 4 5 6 7 8 9 10

9. [paste picture here] 1 2 3 4 5 6 7 8 9 10

# Addition

Use the math picture to count and write the number in each box. Add the numbers.

**1.**
| paste picture here |
| paste picture here | + |

**2.**
| paste picture here |
| paste picture here | + |

**3.**
| paste picture here |
| paste picture here | + |

**4.**
| paste picture here |
| paste picture here | + |

**5.**
| paste picture here |
| paste picture here | + |

**6.**
| paste picture here |
| paste picture here | + |

**7.**
| paste picture here |
| paste picture here | + |

**8.**
| paste picture here |
| paste picture here | + |

**9.**
| paste picture here |
| paste picture here | + |

*Instant & Interactive Math Picture Pages With Activities*
Scholastic Professional Books

# Subtraction

Use the math picture to count and write the number in each box. Subtract the numbers.

**1.**

| paste picture here | |
|---|---|
| paste picture here | − |

**2.**

| paste picture here | |
|---|---|
| paste picture here | − |

**3.**

| paste picture here | |
|---|---|
| paste picture here | − |

**4.**

| paste picture here | |
|---|---|
| paste picture here | − |

**5.**

| paste picture here | |
|---|---|
| paste picture here | − |

**6.**

| paste picture here | |
|---|---|
| paste picture here | − |

**7.**

| paste picture here | |
|---|---|
| paste picture here | − |

**8.**

| paste picture here | |
|---|---|
| paste picture here | − |

**9.**

| paste picture here | |
|---|---|
| paste picture here | − |

# Money

Circle the money you need to pay for each item.

**1.**

| paste picture here |

**2.**

| paste picture here |

**3.**

| paste picture here |

**4.**

| paste picture here |

**5.**

| paste picture here |

*Instant & Interactive Math Picture Pages With Activities*
Scholastic Professional Books

# Multiplication

Use the math picture to count and write the number in each box. Multiply the numbers.

**1.**
paste picture here

paste picture here

X

**2.**
paste picture here

paste picture here

X

**3.**
paste picture here

paste picture here

X

**4.**
paste picture here

paste picture here

X

**5.**
paste picture here

paste picture here

X

**6.**
paste picture here

paste picture here

X

**7.**
paste picture here

paste picture here

X

**8.**
paste picture here

paste picture here

X

**9.**
paste picture here

paste picture here

X

# Graphing

Use the math picture to count the number of each item. Color the graph to show how many of each item you count. Use a different color for each bar.

| | | | | | | | | | |
|---|---|---|---|---|---|---|---|---|---|
**10**
**9**
**8**
**7**
**6**
**5**
**4**
**3**
**2**
**1**

| paste picture here | paste picture here | paste picture here | paste picture here | paste picture here | paste picture here | paste picture here | paste picture here | paste picture here | paste picture here |

*Instant & Interactive Math Picture Pages With Activities*
Scholastic Professional Books

# Character Lists

### School Store
10 pencils
9 boxes of crayons
8 erasers
7 scissors
6 glues bottles
5 marker packs
4 pencil boxes
3 pads
2 notebooks
1 paint set

### Ocean Life
10 lobsters
9 octopuses
8 manatees
7 dolphins
6 porpoises
5 walruses
4 sharks
3 sea lions
2 seals
1 killer whale

### Halloween Party
10 bats
9 witches
8 skeletons
7 spiders
6 ghosts
5 mice
4 Frankensteins
3 pumpkins
2 cats
1 owl

### Rain Forest
10 butterflies
9 tapirs
8 howler monkees
7 sloths
6 snakes
5 toucans
4 frogs
3 lizards
2 anteaters
1 jaguar

### Autumn Harvest
10 apples
9 squash
8 corn shocks
7 pumpkins
6 muffins
5 pies
4 Indian corn
3 jugs of cider
2 jars of jelly
1 hay wagon

### Transportation
10 cars
9 trucks
8 bicycles
7 vans
6 school buses
5 planes
4 helicopters
3 ocean liners
2 trains
1 rocket

### Toy Shop
10 bears
9 dolls
8 toy cars
7 soccer balls
6 trains
5 soldiers
4 rocking horses
3 footballs
2 whistles
1 dinosaur

### Food Pyramid
10 bowls of cereal
9 pieces of bread
8 pears
7 bunches of grapes
6 carrots
5 pieces of cheeses
4 pieces of meat
3 milk cartons
2 eggs
1 butter

### Snow Sports
10 skis
9 ski poles
8 ice skates
7 moose
6 snowshoes
5 bears
4 penguins
3 snowboards
2 sleds
1 toboggan

### Dinosaurs
10 Coelophysis
9 Stegosaurus
8 Ankylosaurus
7 Triceratops
6 Trachodon
5 T-Rex
4 Acrocanthosaurus
3 Corythosaurus
2 Brachiosaurus
1 Elasimosaurus

### Insects
10 ants
9 water beetles
8 fireflies
7 butterflies
6 house flies
5 ladybugs
4 praying mantises
3 bees
2 luna moths
1 grasshopper

### Pleasant Pond
10 frogs
9 ducks
8 canoes
7 swings
6 inner tubes
5 beach chairs
4 giraffes
3 horses
2 lions
1 dock

# Answers

## School Store

### Counting and Number Practice, p. 12

□ 1 2 **3** 4 5 6 7 8 9 10
🍶 1 2 3 4 5 **6** 7 8 9 10
📓 1 2 3 4 5 6 7 8 **9** 10
📦 1 2 3 4 **5** 6 7 8 9 10
✂ 1 2 3 4 5 6 **7** 8 9 10
✏ 1 2 3 4 5 6 7 8 9 **10**
📖 1 2 3 **4** 5 6 7 8 9 10
🖊 1 2 3 4 5 6 7 **8** 9 10
📏 **1** 2 3 4 5 6 7 8 9 10
□ 1 **2** 3 4 5 6 7 8 9 10

### Graphing, p. 13

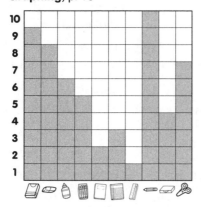

### Addition, p. 14

**1.** 3 + 5 + 8; **2.** 7 + 4 = 11; **3.** 6 + 2 = 8;
**4.** 9 + 2 = 11; **5.** 10 + 1 = 11; **6.** 8 + 3 = 11;
**7.** 4 + 6 = 10; **8.** 5 + 7 = 12; **9.** 9 + 1 = 10

### Subtraction, p. 15

**1.** 7 - 2 = 5; **2.** 9 - 3 = 6; **3.** 10 - 1 = 9; **4.** 9 - 5 = 4;
**5.** 8 - 4 = 4; **6.** 7 - 6 = 1; **7.** 6 - 3 = 3; **8.** 10 - 9 = 1;
**9.** 5 - 2 = 3

## Ocean Life

### Graphing, p. 19

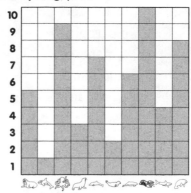

### Addition, p. 20

**1.** 5 + 3 = 8; **2.** 7 + 1 = 8; **3.** 8 + 2 = 10;
**4.** 9 + 4 = 13; **5.** 10 + 3 = 13; **6.** 3 + 8 = 11;
**7.** 7 + 6 = 13; **8.** 2 + 7 = 9; **9.** 4 + 3 = 7

### Subtraction, p. 21

**1.** 9 − 4 = 5; **2.** 8 − 1 = 7; **3.** 10 − 3 = 7;
**4.** 8 − 6 = 2; **5.** 7 − 2 = 5; **6.** 8 − 4 = 4;
**7.** 10 − 4 = 6; **8.** 8 − 2 = 6; **9.** 9 − 6 = 3

### Ocean Life Questions, p. 22

**5.** 55 animals

## Halloween Party

### Graphing, p. 26

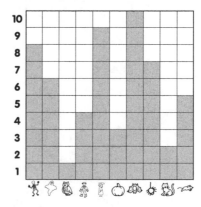

### Addition, p. 27

**1.** 6 + 2 + 4 = 12; **2.** 5 + 7 + 9 = 21;
**3.** 3 + 8 + 2 = 13; **4.** 6 + 5 + 9 = 20;
**5.** 3 + 2 + 4 = 9; **6.** 4 + 10 + 6 = 20

*Instant & Interactive Math Picture Pages With Activities*
Scholastic Professional Books

**Subtraction,** p. 27

**1.** 9 - 2 = 7; **2.** 10 - 3 = 7; **3.** 8 - 6 = 2;
**4.** 9 - 5 = 4; **5.** 7 - 4 = 3; **6.** 10 - 2 = 8;
**7.** 8 - 3 = 5; **8.** 6 - 1 = 5; **9.** 9 - 4 = 5

**Halloween Party Problems,** p. 29

**1.** 3 witches; **2.** 2 ghosts, 3 witches and 2 ghosts;
**3.** 22 shoes; **4.** 13, 14, the witches' and
Frankensteins' team; **5.** First = 3, Second = 2, Third
= 2, 7 in all; **6.** 5 - 3 = 2

# Rain Forest

**Graphing,** p. 33

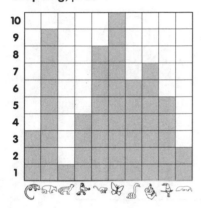

**Addition,** p. 34

**1.** 4 + 5 = 9; **2.** 1 + 9 = 10; **3.** 2 + 10 = 12;
**4.** 3 + 7 = 10; **5.** 9 + 6 = 15; **6.** 4 + 3 = 7;
**7.** 8 + 2 = 10; **8.** 5 + 7 = 12; **9.** 6 + 3 = 9

**Subtraction,** p. 35

**1.** 5 - 4 = 1 **2.** 8 - 1 = 7; **3.** 10 - 3 = 7;
**4.** 7 - 2 = 5; **5.** 9 - 5 = 4; **6.** 6 - 1 = 5;
**7.** 8 - 3 = 5; **8.** 10 - 4 = 6; **9.** 9 - 2 = 7

**Counting by Twos & Fours,** p. 36

**1.** 16; **2.** 4; **3.** 36; **4.** 32; **5.** 8; **6.** 28

# Autumn Harvest

**Addition,** p. 40

**1.** 10 + 2 = 12; **2.** 5 + 4 = 9; **3.** 9 + 1 = 10;
**4.** 6 + 2 = 8; **5.** 3 + 8 = 11; **6.** 5 + 6 = 11;
**7.** 7 + 9 = 16; **8.** 10 + 6 = 16; **9.** 3 + 7 = 10

**Subtraction,** p. 41

**1.** 10 - 3 = 12; **2.** 9 - 5 = 4; **3.** 8 - 2 = 6;
**4.** 5 - 2 = 3; **5.** 7 - 4 = 3; **6.** 9 - 3 = 6;
**7.** 8 - 4 = 4; **8.** 4 - 1 = 3; **9.** 8 - 6 = 2

**Counting Money,** p. 42

Answers will vary.

**Spending Money,** p. 43

Answers will vary.

# Transportation

**Addition,** p. 47

**1.** 5 + 4 = 9; **2.** 2 + 8 = 10; **3.** 6 + 3 = 9;
**4.** 6 + 8 = 14; **5.** 10 + 1 = 11; **6.** 9 + 2 = 11;
**7.** 5 + 9 = 14; **8.** 7 + 4 = 11; **9.** 8 + 6 = 14

**Subtraction,** p. 48

**1.** 10 - 3 = 7; **2.** 6 - 4 = 2; **3.** 9 - 2 = 7;
**4.** 9 - 6 = 3; **5.** 10 - 5 = 5; **6.** 8 - 1 = 7;
**7.** 8 - 2 = 6; **8.** 9 - 7 = 2; **9.** 10 - 6 = 4

**Counting by Twos,** p. 49

**1.** 8; **2.** 2; **3.** 20; **4.** 10; **5.** 6; **6.** 4

**Transportation Questions,** p. 50

**1.** 5 + 4 = 9; **2.** 10 - 8 = 2; **3.** 10 + 7 = 17;
**4.** 5 - 4 = 1; **5.** 2 x 9 = 18; **6.** 5 x 6 = 30; **7.** 28

# Holiday Toy Shop

**Graphing,** p. 54

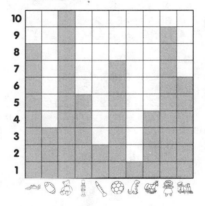

**Addition,** p. 55

**1.** 8 + 2 = 10; **2.** 4 + 7 = 11; **3.** 9 + 10 = 19;
**4.** 1 + 3 = 4; **5.** 5 + 6 = 11; **6.** 8 + 4 = 12;
**7.** 7 + 2 = 9; **8.** 1 + 5 = 6; **9.** 3 + 6 = 9

**Subtraction,** p. 56

**1.** .75 − .42 = .33; **2.** .40 − .10 = .30;
**3.** .50 − .40 = .10; **4.** 1.25 − 1.10 = .15;
**5.** .60 − .50 = .10; **6.** .35 − .20 = .15;

**Holiday Toy Shop Spending,** p. 57

Answers will vary.

## The Food Pyramid

**Addition, p. 61**
Answers will vary.

**Subtraction With Money, p. 62**
**1.** .55 - .40 = .15; **2.** 1.00 - .80 = .20;
**3.** .60 - .50 = .10; **4.** 1.00 - .45 = .55;
**5.** 1.25 - .65 = .60; **6.** .61 - .60 = .01

**Multiplication, p. 63**
**1.** 3 x 6 = 18; **2.** 2 x 4 = 8; **3.** 4 x 8 = 32;
**4.** 3 x 9 = 27; **5.** 2 x 10 = 20; **6.** 2 x 12 = 24;
**7.** 3 x 12 = 36; **8.** 3 x 8 = 24; **9.** 5 x 10 = 50

**Food Pyramid Questions, p. 64**
**6.** 27

## Snow Sports

**Addition, p. 68**
**1.** 5 + 4 + 7 = 16; **2.** 10 + 9 + 2 = 21;
**3.** 8 + 3 + 1 = 12; **4.** 6 + 8 + 2 = 16;
**5.** 8 + 10 + 3 = 21; **6.** 10 + 9 + 3 = 22;
**7.** 10 + 6 + 1 = 17; **8.** 8 + 2 + 1 = 11;
**9.** 3 + 8 + 6 = 17

**Subtraction, p. 69**
**1.** 8 - 1 = 7; **2.** 7 - 5 = 2; **3.** 2 - 1 = 1
**4.** 5 - 4 = 1; **5.** 9 - 3 = 6; **6.** 8 - 6 = 2;
**7.** 10 - 3 = 7; **8.** 7 - 4 = 3; **9.** 9 - 2 = 7

**Multiplication, p. 70**
**1.** 2 x 5 = 10; **2.** 10 x 7 = 70; **3.** 6 x 4 = 24;
**4.** 9 x 4 = 36; **5.** 1 x 5 = 5; **6.** 3 x 7 = 21;
**7.** 3 x 10 = 30; **8.** 6 x 4 = 24; **9.** 9 x 10 = 90

**Snow Sports Questions, p. 71**
**1.** 5 + 7 + 4 = 16; **2.** 10 - 9 = 1;
**3.** 2 + 3 = 5; **4.** 4 x 2 = 8; **5.** 6 x 2 = 12;
**6.** 8 - 3 = 5; **7.** 13 - 3 = 10

## Dinomathic Park – Dinosaurs

**Addition, p. 75**
**1.** 3 + 7 + 4 = 14; **2.** 5 + 9 + 6 = 20;
**3.** 1 + 8 + 6 = 15; **4.** 4 + 7 + 5 = 16;
**5.** 2 + 3 + 9 = 14; **6.** 5 + 9 + 1 = 15

**Measuring, p. 76**
**1.** 15 cm.; **2.** 20 cm.; **3.** 16 cm.; **4.** 20 cm.;
**5.** 2 cm.; **6.** 20 cm.; **7.** 12 cm.; **8.** 10 cm.; **9.** 3 cm.

**Addition, Multiplication & Division p. 77**
Answers will vary.

**Dinomathic Park Questions, p. 78**
**1.** 10 x 10 = 100; **2.** 7 − 5 = 2; **3.** 7 x 5 = 35;
**4.** 9 x 2 = 18; **5.** 9 + 7 = 16; **6.** 8 − 2 = 6

## Insects

**Addition, p. 82**
**1.** 4 + 7 + 5 = 16; **2.** 8 + 2 + 10 = 20;
**3.** 9 + 3 + 8 = 20; **4.** 6 + 4 + 5 = 15;
**5.** 7 + 2 + 3 = 12; **6.** 6 + 9 + 10 = 25

**Measuring, p. 83**
Answers may vary slightly.
**1.** 5 cm ; **2.** 13 cm ; **3.** 10 cm;
**4.** 17 cm; **5.** 6 cm; **6.** 9 cm

**Symmetry, p. 84**

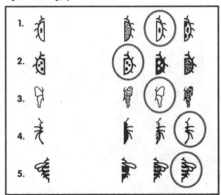

**Insect Questions, p. 85**
**1.** 2 + 7 = 9; **2.** 10 − 5 = 5; **3.** 8 + 3 + 6 = 17;
**4.** 5 x 10 = 50; **5.** 9 x 2 = 18; **6.** 5 pairs; **7.** 45

## Pleasant Pond Park

**Addition, p. 89**
**1.** 8 + 6 = 14; **2.** 10 + 9 = 19; **3.** 3 + 4 = 7;
**4.** 5 + 6 = 11; **5.** 3 + 2 = 5; **6.** 8 + 7 = 15;
**7.** 5 + 7 = 12; **8.** 4 + 2 = 6; **9.** 1 + 8 = 9

**Subtraction, p. 90**
**1.** 7 - 6 = 1; **2.** 9 - 8 = 1; **3.** 10 - 9 = 1;
**4.** 8 - 5 = 3; **5.** 6 - 5 = 1; **6.** 8 - 7 = 1;
**7.** 4 - 2 = 2; **8.** 7 - 3 = 4; **9.** 5 - 1 = 4

**Measuring, p. 91**
Answers may vary slightly.
**1.** 17 cm., 12 cm.; **2.** 5 cm.; **3.** 6 cm., 1 cm.;
**4.** 4 cm.; **5.** 5 cm.; **6.** 8 cm.; **7.** 3 cm., 8 cm.

**Pleasant Pond Park Questions, p. 92**
**1.** .25 x 5 = $1.25; **2.** 9 − 7 = 2;
**3.** 2 x .75 = $1.50, $3.00 - $1.50 = $1.50, Yes;
**4.** 8 x .50 = $4.00; **5.** 10 ÷ 2 = 5, 5 x .50 = $2.50
**6.** 5, 5 x .25 = $1.25; **7.** $1.50

*Instant & Interactive Math Picture Pages With Activities*
Scholastic Professional Books